Coptic Egypt

By the same author:

SAKKARA AND MEMPHIS, A Guide to the Necropolis and the Ancient Capital. Longman, London and New York, 2d ed., 1985.

UPPER EGYPT, Historical Outline and Descriptive Guide to the Ancient Monuments. Longman, London and New York, 1984.

LUXOR, A Guide to Ancient Thebes. Longman, London and New York, 3d ed. 1983.

THE ANCIENT EGYPTIANS, A Popular Introduction to Life in the Pyramid Age. The American University in Cairo Press, 1984.

COPTIC EGYPT

HISTORY AND GUIDE

By
Jill Kamil
Plans and Maps by Hassan Ibrahim

THE AMERICAN UNIVERSITY IN CAIRO PRESS

Dedicated with love to

Timmy and Tawfik

Ricky and Christine

CONTENTS

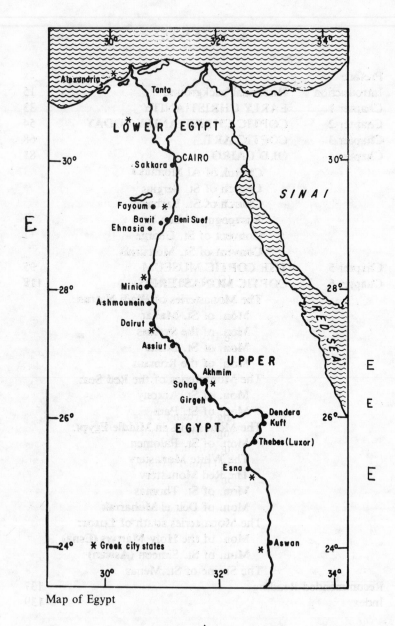

Map of Egypt

ILLUSTRATIONS

PLANS AND MAPS

Coptic cross in ivory inlay on wood panelling. Right altar, Church of St. Sergius, Old Cairo. Photograph by Cassandra Vivian.

PREFACE

The word Copt is derived from the Arabic corruption of the Greek *Aigyptos*, which was, in turn, derived from *Hikaptah*, one of the names for Memphis, the first capital of ancient Egypt. The Arab invaders in the year 640 called Egypt *dar al-Gibt* (home of the Egyptians) and since Christianity was the official religion of Egypt at the time, the word *Gibt* came to refer to the practitioners of Christianity as well as to the inhabitants of the Nile valley.

There has been no Coptic government; the title of this book is used as a cultural expression of the church and the people. The modern use of the term Coptic describes Orthodox Egyptian Christians, as well as the last stage of the ancient Egyptian language, script and liturgy. It describes also the distinctive art and architecture that developed as an early expression of the new faith.

The Coptic Church is based on the teachings of St. Mark who, according to hallowed tradition, brought Christianity to Egypt in the first century. He was one of the four evangelists and author of the oldest canonical gospel. Although integrated into the body politic of the Egyptian nation, the Copts have survived as a strong religious entity who pride themselves on their contribution to the Christian world in the form of monasticism.

Limestone stela in the form of a 'naos' showing a seated child holding a
bunch of grapes and a bird. Provenance unknown. Now in the Coptic
Museum. Photograph courtesy of Coptic Museum.

FOREWORD

It is a pleasure for me to write a foreword to *Coptic Egypt*, which is the first book that provides the reader with a definitive guide to the most frequently visited Coptic monuments throughout Egypt, and includes a separate chapter on the Coptic Museum, which, with its 14,000 objects, represents the largest collection of Coptic art in the world.

Coptology has become an independent discipline only in the last decades. Hitherto, Coptic studies were included, in different universities, in their departments of Graeco-Roman, Near Eastern, or Byzantine studies. Only in 1971 was a Professor of Coptology appointed in Munster University in West Germany; and at other universities, especially in Rome, Geneva and Paris, Coptic studies were limited to the teaching of language and literature.

The general public became more aware of Egypt's Christian heritage when, in 1941, the first exhibition of Coptic art was opened in the United States in the Brooklyn Museum. In 1963 another was opened in West Germany, in Villa Hügel, Essen. These exhibitions familiarised scholars as well as the general public with Coptic art forms, and aroused their interest to know more about this Christian institution. This book will undoubtedly facilitate their understanding and encourage them to visit the sites.

Dr. Gawdat Gabra
Director, Coptic Museum

ACKNOWLEDGMENTS

The author wishes to thank Professor Michael Dols for his suggestions and references concerning the role of the holy man in late antiquity, Professor Ronald Leprohon for reading and commenting on the pharaonic period, Professor John Rodenbeck for help with the Ptolemaic period, and Barbara Ibronyi for her constructive criticism of the chapter on Coptic art, as well as for editing the manuscript.

Special thanks are extended to Dr. Gawdat Gabra, director of the Coptic Museum in Cairo, for help and encouragement, and for permission to take photographs in the Coptic Museum.

INTRODUCTION

Historical Background

Egypt for the first two centuries of our era is an extremely complex, heavily documented, yet poorly understood period of history. The reasons for this are manifold but the most important is that accounts of Egypt in the Middle Ages and the Renaissance were written from the angle of the occupying power and not from the Egyptian point of view. Modern classicists share this prejudice for a number of reasons, one of which is that classical antiquity still provides most of their source material. In other words, Egypt in the early Christian era is presented as a Roman colony, not as a nation with an identity and a tradition that survived Roman occupation. As a result, a sense of continuity has been lost and it is not possible to provide a satisfactory answer to a basic question: how did the Egyptians, with a distinctive civilization, come to accept the divinity of the historical Jesus? Why was Christianity so successful in Egypt?

In order to answer this question, one must go back a thousand years before the Christian era, to the beginning of what is known as the period of decline. Only by tracing this eventful stretch of history, which comprised several distinct phases, can one appreciate the reaction of the people to a unified approach to religion that Christianity offered.

The Last of the Great Pharaohs. Ramses III (1182–1151 BC) was the last of the great pharaohs. He conquered the Libyans and repelled invaders from the north, the People of the Sea, but he and his ever-weakening successors fell more and more under the yoke of the priests of Amon. They had grown increasingly wealthy and wielded great power. There were labour problems and strikes, and finally the high priests seized the throne of Egypt in 1080 BC. Theoretically, the country was still united. In fact, the government became synonymous with corruption and a state of semi-anarchy blighted the land. Occupation by successive foreign military powers was the result.

In 950 BC, Sheshonk, from a family of Libyan descent but completely Egyptianised, took over leadership. The Libyans were probably descendents of mercenary troops who had earlier been granted land in return for military service. The Libyan monarchs conducted themselves as pharaohs and their rule lasted for two centuries.

In 720 BC a military leader from the region of the fourth cataract, Kush (lower Sudan), marched northward. Piankhi did not view himself as a conquerer because his people had absorbed Egyptian culture during a long period of colonial rule. In fact, they felt themselves obliged to free Egypt from the forces of barbarism that they felt had engulfed it. The Egyptians, however, did not regard the Kushites as liberators and it was only after a military clash at Memphis, when the foreigners surged over the ramparts of the ancient city, that the Egyptians surrendered. Like the Libyans before them, the Kushites established themselves as genuine pharaohs, restored ancient temples and were sympathetic to local customs and institutions.

The Assyrians, who bear the reputation of being the most militaristic and ruthless of ancient peoples, conquered Egypt in 671 BC, putting an end to Kushite rule. With a well-trained army they moved south, from province to province, assuring the local population of a speedy liberation from oppression. But the Egyptians rebelled against the new invaders and drove them north again. The Assyrians staged a counter-attack. They scaled the walls of the ancient city of Memphis and took it by force. Realising that occupation of Upper Egypt was necessary for the complete pacification of the country they marched southward again, this time desecrating monuments, killing people and looting temples.

After these long centuries of foreign rule Egypt knew but one short respite: a brilliant revival, which is called the Saite Period,

16

when an Egyptian named Psamtik liberated the country from Assyrian occupation in 664 BC. He turned his attention to reuniting Egypt, establishing order and promoting Egyptian tradition.

Monarchical rule was by tradition highly personal. The god-king, the personification of *maat* (an abstract concept referring to order and justice), was spokesman of the gods. He heard appeals and granted petitions. A strong leader had power: he was responsible for the economy of the country. He had military strength to repell Egypt's enemies, and he exercised *maat*, which was based on the concept of cosmic order. Years of occupation had, however, shattered the confidence of the people in the pharaoh. Their inherent trust and optimism faltered.

When one thinks of ancient Egypt, its great temples and national ritual, one does not think of personal piety. There is, however, evidence for the relationship between the two. Texts leave no doubt that ordinary people went to national temples to bring their private problems before their local god. Some important officials and sages, as well as high priests who raised statues in temple precincts, were regarded as intermediaries in approaching the deity. "Say a prayer on my behalf" or "invoke my name" are frequent phrases left beside such statues by people who journeyed to the temple for the express purpose of submitting personal entreaties. Statuary thus played a part as a point of contact in worship.

It is important to note, in view of Christianity's stress on humility, that evidence of personal piety had extended to all levels of society centuries earlier: the workers' community at Deir el-Medina on the Theban necropolis, for example, had monuments containing such phrases as "poor in spirit," "look upon me and be merciful" and "punish me not for my many sins." And the piety of the pharaoh can be seen in relief: in the temple of Seti I, at Abydos, he is shown in numerous representations bending slightly at the waist in reverence before an honoured deity. This is a far cry from the all-powerful pharaoh who was, himself, a god.

Respect for kingship was reinstated by Psamtik. The unflagging efforts of this great leader, and the Saite rulers that followed him, to restore order and former greatness led them to pattern their

17

government, religion and society on the Old Kingdom, a civilisation that was already two thousand years old. Instead of chanelling their energies into new forms, they fell back on the past. This conservative policy of the Saite rulers helped to earn for Egypt the reputation it has long borne, of being a civilisation devoid of creativity, philosophy and individuality. This reputation, as we shall shortly see, was far from deserved.

Egypt's revival came to an end when the Persian king Cambyses occupied the land in 525 BC and turned Egypt into a Persian province. The new rulers, like the Libyans and the Kushites before them, at first showed respect for the religion and customs of the country in an effort to gain support. But the Egyptians were not deceived. As soon as an opportunity arose, they routed their invaders. Unfortunately, they were able only to maintain independence for about sixty years before the Persian army reconquered Egypt. This time there was less tolerance of local customs.

The Greeks at this time were entering their classical period and making their presence felt throughout the Mediterranean world. Communications between Egypt and the Greek states were becoming more frequent and among the Greek scholars who came to Egypt before Alexander the Great were: Thales of Miletus, the statesman and scientist; Pythagoras the philosopher and mathematician; Solon the politician and lawyer; Hecataeus of Miletus, who wrote the first systematic description of the world; and, finally, Herodotus the traveller historian, who devoted the second of his nine books on history to Egypt. Herodotus gathered information (sometimes from unreliable sources) about the land and the people. He described how Egyptian temples were plundered by the Persians and how Cambyses, in a fit of anger, killed the sacred Apis bull as well as a large number of Egyptians. Little wonder that when Alexander the Great came to Egypt in 332 BC, he and his army were welcomed by the Egyptians. At least they shared a mutual hatred of the Persians. When Alexander consulted the oracle of Amon, at Siwa Oasis, he authenticated his leadership and was recognised as the legitimate successor to the ancient pharaohs.

Ptolemaic Rule of Egypt. Before he left Egypt, Alexander laid down the basic plans for its government. He was quick to realise the benefits of leaving to trained Egyptians the task that they had carried on for thousands of years, especially with the assessment and collection of taxes. In order to do this, he accepted the Egyptian divisions of the country into different provinces, (*nomes* in Greek), each under an Egyptian governor (*nomarchs*); he also laid out the plans for his great city and seaport, Alexandria, so situated as to facilitate the flow of Egypt's surplus resources to the archipelago, and also to intercept all trade with Africa and Asia.

When Alexander met his untimely death of a fever at Babylon, the great Macedonian empire declined. Egypt was held by General Ptolemy, who gradually took over leadership first as satrap, then governor and, finally, in 305 BC, as king Ptolemy I. During the three centuries of Ptolemaic rule that followed, Egypt became, for the first time in a thousand years, the seat of a brilliant kingdom once more and a Greek-Egyptian culture emerged. It is important to stress the *Egyptian* element because it provides the link, the historical continuity we shall trace in the early Christian era.

Ptolemy did not continue Alexander's practice of founding cities. In fact, with the exception of Ptolemais, on the western bank of the Nile in Middle Egypt (which he named after himself) and the old Greek city of Naucratis, in the Delta, only Alexandria represented a traditional Greek city-state. Ptolemy chose, instead, to settle his mercenary troops (Greeks, Macedonians, Persians, and Hellenised Asiatics) among the Egyptian population, in or near the capitals of the provinces. Although these were towns of some considerable size, they had no self-government and were probably regarded, by the Greeks, as not much more than villages, despite the designation *polis*: Hermopolis, 'the city of Hermes' (modern Ashmounein), for example, and Hierakleopolis, 'the city of Heracles' (modern Ehnasia), to the south of the Fayoum. In the Fayoum, a fertile depression in the western desert, the bulk of Ptolemy's troops were pensioned with large tracts of land. Many of the settlers married Egyptians and, by the second and third generations,

19

their children bore both Greek or Egyptian names, just as Egyptians, like Manetho, adopted Greek names. It is important to allude to this because when we approach the Christian era, the names mentioned in ecclesiastical literature are all Greek. This gives the erroneous impression that Egyptians played no part in the theological discussions that lay in the future.

In Alexandria Greeks formed the bulk of the population, followed in number by the Jews. But there was also a large Egyptian population which lived west of the city, in the old quarter of Rhacotis. Alexandria occupied the strip of sandy soil between Lake Mareotis and the sea, where the island of Pharos with its the famous lighthouse was built. The island, when artificially connected with the mainland, resulted in a spacious harbour being formed on the east; and a few miles further east was Canopus, which became a popular Greek tourist city.

Ptolemy I introduced a cult designed to provide a link between his subjects, Greek and Egyptian. He observed that the Apis bull was worshipped at Memphis, which was even then a thriving religious centre, and he assumed, wrongly, that the cult was popular and widespread. The deceased Apis was known as Osiris-Apis, or 'Oserapis', from which Serapis was derived. It is presumed that Ptolemy supplied Serapis with anthropomorphic features and declared it to be national god. To launch the new deity on his career, Ptolemy declared that he had had a dream in which a colossal statue was revealed to him. No sooner did he communicate his revelation to the people, than a statue of Serapis was put on view, closely resembling his vision: a man with curly hair, a benign expression and a long beard. The cult of Serapis was to have sweeping success throughout Greece and Asia Minor, in Sicily, and especially in Rome. But in Egypt Serapis was never worshipped outside of Alexandria and Memphis, where, on the necropolis of Sakkara, the temple of Serapis, the Serapeum, became one of the most famous sites in Egypt.

However, Egypt's other deities were also identified with those of Greece. The god at Thebes, Amon-Ra, was identified with Zeus, supreme god of Olympus, and Amon's wife, Mut, with Hera, Zeus' consort and queen of the sky. The Egyptian Horus was easily identified with Apollo, both being sun-gods. Thoth, the Egyptian god of wisdom said to have invented writing, was associated with Hermes, messenger of Zeus. Osiris, god of the underworld, became one with Hades of the Greek underworld, while Isis, beloved wife of Osiris and mother of Horus, was identified with the earth-mother Demeter. This pantheon of gods enabled the Egyptians and Egyptianised Greeks to worship the same gods in the same temples, under different names. When Ptolemy II started construction of the Temple of Isis on Philae, an island in the Nile south of Aswan, it became a popular healing centre and the cult of Isis swept the Mediterranean world.

Alexandria became capital in place of Memphis, and was soon to become the greatest seat of learning in the Mediterranean world. Ptolemy II commissioned Egyptians to translate their literature into Greek, and a priest called Manetho wrote the history of his country. Ptolemy III issued a decree that all travellers disembarking at Alexandria should have taken from them, in exchange for an official certified copy, any literature in their baggage. Research, especially with practical aims, was fostered and distinguished astronomers, mathematicians, geographers, historians, poets and philosophers gravitated to the Museum attached to the Library, which was a research institution. Among the famed scientists who worked in Alexandria were Eratosthenes, the great geographer of antiquity, who measured the circumference of the earth to within fifty miles; Euclid, author of the *Elements*, the text book that remained standard until the beginning of this century; and Archimedes the mathematician and mechanist, inventor among other things of the Archimedian Screw which is still used for irrigation in Egypt today.

The Ptolemies regarded Egypt as their land and they played a dual role in it, conducting themselves as both Greeks and "legitimate" kings of Egypt. The roles were separate, yet interrelated. As Greeks they resided in Alexandria, the great intellectual centre; yet, as pharaohs they lavished revenues on local priesthoods for the upkeep of temples or at least exempted them from taxes.

21

Architects and artists tackled the task of construction and restoration with vigor. The temples were built on traditional lines, often on the sites of more ancient temples. The walls were adorned with scenes depicting Ptolemaic kings in the manner of the ancient pharaohs, duly equipped with names and titles in hieroglyphics. Like the ancient pharaohs, they assumed religious office and made ceremonial journeys up the Nile to make offerings at these temples. Public worship of political leadership that was a feature of the central religious organisation that had long existed in Egypt, and the Ptolemies were ready to accept symbolic acts of homage by the Egyptians if it pleased them. Indeed, one aspect of the power of the pharaoh was his capacity to uphold religious order, and the Ptolemies thus continued an ancient tradition. In their conscientious provision for temples, they not only maintained the Egyptian sense of prestige, but also helped ensure the continuation of both ancient rituals and the class of priests, scribes and scholars who carried forward Egyptian thought and tradition.

Bilingual Egyptians realised long before the conquest by Alexander that if they transcribed their own language into the Greek alphabet, which was well known among the middle classes and was simpler to read than demotic — the cursive form of hieroglyphics in its latest development — communication would be easier. Scribes started transliterating Egyptian sounds into the Greek alphabet, adding seven extra letters from the Egyptian alphabet to accommodate the extra sounds for which there were no Greek letters. The emergence of this new script, now known as Coptic, cannot be dated precisely. The earliest attempt to write the Egyptian language alphabetically in Greek, feeble but important, has survived in an inscription dating to the Kushite dynasty (750–656 BC) at Abydos; and there was a time when Coptic and demotic were used simultaneously. Demotic Instruction Literature for example, survived well into the Roman period, and demotic graffiti have been found in the Temple of Isis at Philae that date to as late as AD 452, a time when widespread use of script other than Coptic had long died out.

Greek also became the mother-tongue of the Jews in Egypt, who constituted the second largest foreign community. They had established sizable communities since their expulsion from Jerusalem by Nebuchadnezzar in 685 BC, and had settlements even as far south as the island of Elephantine opposite Aswan. When Palestine had fallen under the control of King Ptolemy I in 301 BC, he had brought back Jewish mercenaries who joined the already established communities. Unable to speak Hebrew, which had disappeared as a living language, Egyptian Jews soon felt a need to translate their sacred books into Greek. According to legend seventy-two translators were chosen from among the most learned Jewish scholars, and the resulting version of the Old Testament written in Alexandria is known as *the Septuagint* and is the basis of biblical translations into every European language.

In view of centuries of contact between Egyptians and Jews in Egypt, it is not surprising that some cultural diffusion is evidence in the Old Testament. It can be seen in names such as Pinehas and Pashur, which derive from the Egyptian *pa nhsy* (the Negro) abd *ps-Hr* (part of Horus), respectively, as well as in references to Egypt's indiginous plans, and Egyptian materials such as linen and natron. There are striking resemblances in Biblical and Egyptian expression and imagery. For example, an Egyptian sage called Amenemope (c.1320–1080 BC), whose works were widely distributed, admonished: "Set thyself in the arms of God," while Moses blessed: "The eternal God is a dwelling place, and underneath are the everlasting arms;" "Yahweh weigheth the hearts" is written in Proverb 21:2 and it has not passed unobserved that the only doctrine in which a god weighs the human heart is in the court of Osiris in the underworld, where it is weighed against the feather of truth; the biblical description of men being fashioned out of clay by Yahweh is similar to the ancient Egyptian image of men being fashioned on a potter's wheel out of clay from the river Nile by the god Khnum; finally, the analogies between the Book of Proverbs and the words of Amenemope are beyond doubt, and indicate direct borrowing.

A collection of syncretistic treatises known as the *Corpus Hermeticum* (Hermetic literature) circulated widely in Alexandria in Ptolemaic times. The corpus was purportedly written by Thoth, the ancient Egyptian god of wisdom who, under his Greek name Hermes Trismegistus, gave the compilation its name. The Hermetic texts were a blend of Greek philosophy, ancient Egyptian wisdoms, esoteric teachings, cosmological conceptions and mysticism. In other words, it comprised the writings of pagan intellectuals, Egyptians and Greeks. The Hermetic literature included magic and because of this it was later to be forbidden to Christians. The texts were 'hermetically' sealed. Clement, one of the early church fathers, nevertheless wrote positively about the texts, which he said contained forty-two sacred revelations of Hermes and constituted the entire range of material available, geographical and medical works included, for the education of Egyptian priests. The *Hermetica* that has been handed down to us originated in Roman times in corrupted form from numerous translations. The author of the original work (if, indeed, it was the product of a single mind) was regarded in late antiquity as a great teacher. Plato wrote about him as a 'man of letters', transcribing his name as 'Theuth'. The reference to Thoth's authorship was probably based on ancient Egyptian tradition of Thoth being the god of wisdom, and forty-two being the number of Egyptian provinces. This implies that the sacred writings, a synthesis of the Egyptian and Greek heritages, were known throughout the land.

The Ptolemies encouraged foreigners to come and live in Egypt. The immigrants included Semites, Syrians and Persians, as well as Greeks, who took up residence in the Delta, in certain quarters of Memphis, and the Fayoum where an enormous settlement grew up. When these cosmopolitan communities are considered in addition to the upper class Greeks and their officials, who resided in Alexandria and the Greek city-states, and the thousands of Greek and Macedonian soldiers, merchants and businessmen, it can be readily seen that Egypt, prior to the Christian era, was inhabited by an extremely diversified population. The complex society was superimposed on an already highly stratified Egyptian society that ranged from learned literates to the peasant masses.

There was a strong anti-Egyptian feeling among the sophisticated Greeks, who did not encourage Egyptians to become citizens of

Alexandria and the Greek cities. Further, although they held the Egyptian culture in reverence in many ways, they did not learn the Egyptian language or writing. Even the Greek masses, fascinated by the 'sacred mysteries' and 'divine oracles' of the Land of Wonders, nevertheless held the Egyptians in contempt. Papyri found in the Greek cities, which provide a wealth of documentary evidence of how such communities lived, clearly reflect disdain for the Egyptians.

There was also an anti-Greek feeling among the Egyptians, who had a strong sense of cultural superiority to anyone who did not speak their language. Herodotus had remarked on this attitude even in Persian times. Although there is evidence that Egyptian priests and officials collaborated with the Ptolemies, there is also evidence that they rebelled frequently, resentful of the fact that they were treated as a conquered race. Prophetic writings were widely circulated among the Egyptians promising the expulsion of the foreigners. One Upper Egyptian province in particular, the Thebaid (Luxor), remained the most ardently nationalistic. The Ptolemies' unequal treatment of their subjects led to ever more frequent Egyptian revolts. Progressively diminishing respect for the ruling power was such that Ptolemy VI (170 BC), whose papers formed a large part of the papyri housed in the Serapeum in Alexandria until the middle of the second century, complained bitterly of attacks made on him "because I am a Greek." Amusing evidence of the Egyptian sense of superiority is expressed in a text in which Egyptians were instructed, after having cursed the head of a sacrificial lamb, either to cast it into the Nile or sell it to the Greeks.

Towards the end of the second century BC there were economic problems and unrest in Egypt, along with a decline in foreign commerce resulting from the loss, by Ptolemy VI, of Egypt's Syrian possessions to Philip of Macedon and Antiochus of Syria. The last of the Ptolemies were weak leaders and the prosperity of the kingdom declined. The court, rich in material wealth and lax in morals, became the scene of decadence and anarchy.

It is interesting to note that centuries before the Christian era there is evidence of men of piety renouncing worldly concerns and

25

devoting themselves to lives of spiritual contemplation and prayer. This occurred in Egypt, where they lived in places of strict seclusion in the desert and in ancient tombs, in Palestine, in caves near the Dead Sea, and further east in Persia and India. The Greeks called the hermits anchorites (derived from the Greek root to 'retire' or 'withdraw'). The term originally referred to those who withdrew from labour, but soon came to describe anti-materialistic ascetics who lived in isolated seclusion.

By the last century of Ptolemaic rule the Egyptians had acquired a position that was somewhat nearer equality with the Greeks than they had enjoyed under the earlier Ptolemies; in fact Egyptian veterans received allotments of land like the Greeks, which may have been made possible as a result of rival claimants to the throne rallying among the native population for popular support. It is important to note the emergence of a landed, wealthy Egyptian segment of the population because they were ardently nationalistic, had little respect for the settlers, were to suffer most severely under the Romans and, finally, it was from their ranks that some of Coptic Christianity's great spiritual leaders were to arise.

Cleopatra IX, a figure of world-wide fame, came to the throne at the age of about eighteen, as co-regent with her younger brother Ptolemy XIII. They were at that time under the guardianship of the Roman Senate. The Romans interferred in the rivalry between them, which led Ptolemy to banish his sister from Egypt. Cleopatra sought refuge in Syria with a view to raising an army and recovering the throne by force of arms. When the ageing Julius Caesar came to Alexandria in 47 BC, he took the side of the banished queen, set her on the throne, and Cleopatra bore his only son, Caesarion.

Mark Antony, Caesar's close friend, fell in love with Cleopatra and spent years of debauchery with her. He was eventually declared by the Roman Senate to be an enemy of his country and Octavianus marched against him, defeating him at Actium, and capturing Alexandria. Antony committed suicide, and Cleopatra, the last monarch to wear the crown bearing the sacred uraeus, the cobra symbolising kingship, and to bear the title Lord of the Two Lands, is also

26

said to have caused her own death by the bite of an asp. Caesarion, her son, who had been coregent since 43 BC, was murdered, and Octavianus became sole ruler of Egypt in 30 BC.

Roman Occupation of Egypt. From the beginning of Roman rule in Egypt there were pitched battles from Alexandria to Thebes. Although the Roman emperors claimed to be successors of the ancient pharaohs, as had the Greeks before them, it is clear that the Egyptians did not regard them as such. Not only did they live in far off Rome and appoint a prefect, or representative, to the position formerly held in the scheme of government by the kings, but the prefect did not perform the ceremonial functions of divine kingship. There was, therefore, a drastic change in the climate of leadership. Augustus made the mistake of arousing the ire of the Greeks in Alexandria when he abolished the Greek Senate and took administrative powers from Greek officials. Further, in response to an appeal by Herod, king of Judea, to restore to his people the land that had been bestowed on Cleopatra during her short refuge in Syria, he not only agreed to that request but also agreed to grant self-government to the Hellenised Jews of Alexandria. This caused great consternation among the Greeks, who had founded the city and had distrusted Roman ambition from the beginning. Their formal request to Augustus to retract the privileges granted the Jews was ignored. Fighting soon broke out, first between Greeks and Jews, then with Roman participation when they tried to separate the two. The unrest that marks the beginning of the Christian era in Alexandria had already begun. Ships in the harbour were set on fire, the flames spread to the Museum, and the main Library in the palace was burned. An estimated 490,000 rolls of papyrus perished.

The Romans thenceforth stationed garrisons at Alexandria, which remained the capital, at Babylon (Old Cairo), which was the key to communications with Asia and with Lower Egypt, and at Syene (Aswan), which was Egypt's southern boundary. They controlled Egypt by force, and regarded the land as no more than a granary supplying wheat to Rome. Consequently, an enormous burden of taxation was placed on the people of the Nile valley. A

27

census was imposed on villages throughout the land and house-to-house registration of the number of residents was made, which might have been considered normal procedure in Rome, but was regarded as an infringement on their privacy by Egyptians. Calculations of the wheat quota were based not on the productivity of the land but on the number of men in a village.

Egyptians who had enjoyed certain privileges under the later Ptolemies and acquired considerable wealth received no special consideration by the Romans. Indeed, they had their problems compounded when the Emperor Trajan declared that peasant farmers should be recruited for the Roman army. Hadrian reduced rentals on imperial lands, exempted citizens of Greek cities from taxation, and also Greek settlers in the Fayoum; but the Egyptian rural population was assessed at a flat rate, without regard for income, age or capacity for work. When men fled or hid, the Romans discovered a cruel way to coerce their families to reveal their whereabouts; aware of the value set by the Egyptians on proper mummification and internment of their dead, they seized bodies and held them ransom. Such evidence dates from the reigns of the emperors Caligua and Claudius in the first half of the first century. By the time of the emperor Nero, 54–68, there are records of men having "fled leaving no property," forty-three in number, then sixty, then a hundred from a single village.

The Romans made an overt show of respect for Egyptian priesthoods by constructing new or completing older temples built by the Ptolemies; the temple to the goddess Hathor at Dendera, for example, which was started under the later Ptolemies, was completed some 185 years later under the emperor Tiberius. And temples in the traditional style were completed at Esna, Kom Ombo, and Philae. It is worthy of note, however, that the sites for these temples were chosen for their strategic position as well as for the sake of ancient tradition. Esna had been a centre for local commerce from earliest times; Kom Ombo, situated on a hill, commanded the trade routes to Nubia in the south; and Philae was situated on Egypt's southern border.

Temple lands elsewhere, however, were annexed and placed under the control of the Roman government. Local priests were allotted only a small part of sacred property and their own material wealth was curbed. The produce of vineyards, palm groves, and fig plantations owned by temples was collected by Roman officials and taxes were levied on sheep, oxen, horses and donkeys. A Roman official held the title of High Priest of Alexandria and all Egypt and was the supreme authority over all the temples.

The institution of sacrosanct monarchy, a cardinal feature of Egyptian life that had existed in pharaonic times and had been maintained by various later dynasties, was lost in Roman times. The emperors may have claimed to be divine but it was their prefects who ruled Egypt, reduced the prestige of the priests and exerted pressure on the people. They siphoned off the wealth of the land to Rome and even recruited Egyptians to fight Roman wars in other countries.

It is not difficult to see the difference between Ptolemaic and Roman rule in Egypt. Under the Ptolemies, Egypt had retained its integrity and had had a stable economy. Under the Romans, the country was shorn of identity and impoverished. It was no more than a private estate of the emperor and a pleasure-ground for the Roman upper classes, who visited Egypt in vast numbers. Romans travelled in luxurious Nile cruises to see the Pyramids of Giza, one of the seven wonders of the ancient world, and visiting such attractions as the statue of Amenhotep III on the Theban necropolis (that they called the Colossus of Memnon because at dawn each day it gave off strange sounds that they interpreted as Memnon, the legendary son of Aurora, greeting his mother), and healing centres such as Deir el-Bahri and the Temple of Isis on Philae.

The cult of Egypt's most beloved goddess Isis exerted a strong influence on the early church, and particularly on Coptic Christianity. The Osiris myth is, therefore, considered worthy of note. It is one of the most poignant, and probably the most well-known of ancient Egypt. Surviving in oral tradition and variably recounted over the centuries, it has come down to us in many versions and with many contradictions. The most complete version is given by Plutarch, the Greek writer who visited Egypt towards the end of

29

the Ptolemaic period. The main theme of the myth is as follows:

Osiris, with his devoted wife Isis at his side, had been a just ruler who was slain by his jealous brother Set. His body was sealed in a chest and thrown into the Nile. The broken-hearted Isis eventually found the body of her husband and laid it beneath a tamarisk bush. However, Set was out boar-hunting, found it and cut it into fourteen pieces, scattering it in all directions. Isis again went in search of Osiris' body, this time with the aid of her sister, the goddess Nepthys. They collected the pieces and, with the aid of the jackal-god of embalmment, Anubis, prepared Osiris for burial. Meanwhile Isis wept and prayed and chanted magical incantations, "making a shadow with her pinions, causing a wind with her wings, raising the weary limbs of the silent-hearted (i.e. Osiris), receiving his seed and bringing forth an heir. . . . "

When Isis gave birth to a son, Horus, she was obliged to hide him until he grew to manhood. The tales of Isis' devotion to her son Horus were many and varied. She brought him up secretly in the marshes in the Delta until he was strong. Then Horus set out in search of Set, his father's slayer, and many and terrible were the battles between them. Horus, however, triumphed over evil and emerged as victor. Egyptian mortuary literature is full of references to the faithful wife seeking the body of her husband. The weeping and lamentations of Isis and her sister Nepthys for Osiris were a widespread expression of sorrow to the Egyptians. They loved to dwell on the loyalty and devotion of Isis, the piety of Horus who triumphed over evil, and the beloved ruler, Osiris, who was killed but who rose to rule again.

The cults Isis and Serapis spread throughout the Graeco-Roman world. Although the Roman Republic at first tried to suppress the Isis cult and its esoteric mysteries, they were unsuccessful. Vespasian (69–79) finally permitted, though did not encourage, the worship of the Egyptian goddess in Rome. The annual festival of Isis (*navigium Isidis*) was celebrated there, even under Christian emperors, until the fourth century. In Egypt, the Temple of Isis on Philae remained a focal point of worship until the reign of Justinian (527–565).

30

Wood inlay altar screen and icons. Church of St. Sergius, Old Cairo.
Photograph by Cassandra Vivian.

31

Stairway to the Nile at the point where the Holy Family is supposed to have begun its journey to Upper Egypt. Church of the Blessed Virgin, Maadi. Photograph by Cassandra Vivian.

1

EARLY CHRISTIANITY

According to honoured tradition Saint Mark brought Christianity to Egypt in the reign of the Roman emperor Nero in the first century. Some of the earliest converts to the new faith undoubtedly came from within the Jewish community in Egypt, which represented the largest concentration outside of Palestine. In fact, tradition also holds that Saint Mark's first convert was a Jewish shoemaker in the Mediterranean capital.

Christianity spread throughout Egypt within half a century of Saint Mark's arrival in Alexandria as is clear from New Testament writings found in Bahnasa, in Middle Egypt, which date around the year 200, and a fragment of the Gospel of Saint John, written in Coptic, which was found in Upper Egypt and can be dated to the first half of the second century.

Evidence of the diffusion of the new faith in the early centuries is, nevertheless, scanty. This holds true not for Egypt alone but all over the Roman world. One of the reasons may be attributed to the need to conceal any connection with the persecuted sect. Another, to the fact that official documents did not require mention of religious affiliation. However, an Egyptian text written in demotic, known as the Insinger Papyrus (now in Leiden), has survived. It dates to the first century and shows that there is not, as is generally supposed, an unbridgeable abyss between pharaonic (pagan) Egypt and the early Christian period. The Insinger Papyrus is of the genre of ancient Egyptian Instruction Literature, and is believed to be a collection of popular works transmitted in numerous copies. It shows that the Egyptians, even after the loss of their independence and centuries of foreign rule, continued to believe in, and to teach, an all-embracing cosmic order which governed human existence. It is fitting to quote the text at the beginning of this chapter, because

33

it shows the Egyptian conception of God, written in their own script, during the crucial period when Christianity was spreading in Egypt. In other words, it provides evidence of the stream of traditional thought in late antiquity. These are selections from the twenty-fourth instruction, "The teaching of knowing the greatness of the god, so as to put it in your heart":

> When people raise their hands the god knows it.
> He knows the impious man who thinks of evil.
> He knows the godly man and that he has the greatness of god in his heart.
> He gives good judgement through the counsel which no one knows.
> He creates abundant value without there being a storehouse behind him.
> It is he who makes the way safe without there being a guard.
> It is he who gives the just law without there being a judgement.
> The hidden work of the god, he makes it known on the earth daily.
> He created light and darkness . . .
> He created the earth, begetting millions . . .
> He created day, month, year . . .
> He created summer and winter . . .
> He created food before those who are alive, the wonder of the fields.
> He created the breath in the egg where there is no access to it.
> He created sleep to end weariness.
> He created remedies to end illness.
>
> Great is the council of the god in putting one thing after another.
> The fate and fortune that come, it is the god who sends

them. (Papyrus Insinger, *Ancient Egyptian Literature,* Lichtheim, M., Vol III, p. 184 ff.).

The first important institution of religious learning in Christian
antiquity was the Catechetical School of Alexandria. It was founded
by Pantanaeus, a Christian scholar who is believed to have come
to Alexandria about 180 and founded the school ten years later. Its
scope was not limited to theological subjects, because science, math-
ematics and the humanities were also taught there. Significantly,
the emergence of the school coincides with the first direct attacks
by the Romans on the Christians of Alexandria.

Clement (160–215), a convert from paganism who succeeded
Pantaneous, was an early apostle of Christian liberalism. He taught
in Alexandria for more than twenty years. He wrote positively about
the Hermetic literature but was bitterly critical of the gnostics (from
the Greek *gnosis* or 'knowledge') and 'their heresies.' Clement was
succeeded by Origen who was of 'pure Coptic stock' and regarded
as the greatest of the early Christian apologists. He joined the
Catechetical School at an early age, attended lectures by Pantaneous
and Clement, and later taught there for twenty-eight years. Like
Clement, he was highly critical of the gnostic movement, which
seemed to be spreading as quickly as Christianity.

The origin of the gnostic communities is obscure and until recently not much was known about them. The reason is that when, in
the fourth century, the gnostics were hounded into silence in the
name of orthodox Christianity, their writings were destroyed whenever they could be found. Consequently, vital evidence on the early
dissemination of the Christian faith among such communities is
lacking. Fortunately, a collection of manuscripts bound into codices, or books, was discovered in Nag Hammadi in Upper Egypt
in 1945. These texts have raised important issues about the development of Christianity in Egypt. They are copied from original writings that cannot be dated with certainty, but may date from as early
as the second half of the first century.

The twelve Nag Hammadi codices, or the Nag Hammadi library

as it is now known, was collected by Egyptians and translated into Coptic, the Egyptian language of the time. They vary widely in content presenting a syncretic spectrum of heritages: local Egyptian concepts and folklore, ancient literature and mystery cults of the Graeco-Roman world, Greek philosophy, Persian mysticism, the Old and the New Testament. The codices include: The Gospel of Thomas; a compilation of sayings attributed to Jesus, in the opening passage of which is the claim that the words were spoken by the living (post-resurrection) Jesus to Thomas Didymus Judas; extracts from Plato's *Republic*; and apocryphons (literally "secret books") on Zoroaster and Manichaeism (named after its founder whose syncretistic religion drew on Zoroastrianism and Christianity). The Persian doctrines were first brought to Egypt by Manichaen missionaries in the second century and it was not long before the teachings of Mani spread beyond Alexandria to the Fayoum and then to Upper Egypt. Little wonder that the Gnostics came under violent attack by both the defenders of Greek philosophy and by orthodox Christians. Already the codices have revealed that the movement was not only far more widespread than was previously thought but of greater historical consequence than hitherto supposed.

The library also includes numerous teachings, treatises, revelations, acts and gospels, some hitherto unknown: the Gospel of Philip, the Gospel of Truth, and the Gospel of the Egyptians. In the latter — according to Greek monk Epiphanius in the ninth century — Jesus is supposed to have said to his disciples, 'the same was the Father, the same was the Son and the same the Holy Ghost.' This is interesting to note because the theological controversy that was destined to sever the early Church into the Latin or Roman Church, the Eastern (predominently Greek) Church and the Egyptian Orthodox (Coptic) Church, pivotted on the three beings of the Trinity.

The theological disputes that broke out among Christians concerned the definition of the nature of Jesus, which was of crucial importance to the new religion. It was extremely abstract and concerned such definitions as 'Father', 'Son', 'begotten' and 'unbegotten'. It may have become a critical issue because Christianity attracted people from many backgrounds with different traditions, concepts of godliness, and styles of worship. Both Christianity and pagan philosophy were in a constant process of change and development in the early centuries when material decline was steep and the ferment of religious feelings most intense.

The rapid spread of Christianity was undoubtedly accelerated by the conditions prevailing in Egypt under Roman rule. For example, the emperor Septimus Severus, the military commander who was strong enough to hold together the Roman Empire for nearly two decades, decreed in 202 that municipal councils should be set up in all the *nome* capitals. The purpose, from the point of view of the Romans, may have been to upgrade the status of the Egyptians and, hopefully, make them more responsible. But Egyptians saw the measure as restrictive, and resisted it. Consequently, they were severely penalised. This led to threats and intimidation. A new wave of brutality started, especially in areas where Roman presence was strongest.

Under the emperor Decius (249–251) Egyptians were ordered to participate in pagan worship in the presence of Roman officers and submit certificates of sacrifice. Those that refused were declared to be self-avowed Christians and they were tortured. The Decian persecution, which was fortunately cut short by the death of the emperor in battle, was the first systematic attempt to put an end to Christianity by depriving the church of both its leaders and followers. Some Christians, in fear for their safety, sent in false certificates. Others managed to escape to the solitude of the desert. But many were willing to die rather than abjure their faith; and their martyrdom further accelerated the Christian movement.

Paul and Antony, two of Egypt's earliest and most well-known spiritual leaders took to a life of meditation and prayer at this time. Each, unknown to the other, chose a site in the eastern desert in a range of mountains near the Gulf of Suez. Ascetic leaders were sometimes of simple origins, like Paul, and sometimes came from among the class of successful landowners, like the family of Antony, who had a certain status in the society. It is important to stress

37

that wealthy land-owners, as well as simple farmers, became hermits because when such people renounced their material possesssions they became regarded as men who had lodged in them a special power and relationship with the divine. By this time thousands of ascetics, whose original models may be traced to pre-Christian times, were either living alone or in small groups. They started to look for guidance from a master, and Paul and Antony gave instruction in an atmosphere of security and spirituality.

In the year 284, the Roman army elected Diocletian emperor. His reforms mark a turning-point in the history of Christianity. The appalling social and economic conditions throughout the Roman Empire led him to drastically reorganise it along military lines. In Egypt he divided the land into three major provinces and separated civic and military powers. Then he imposed new methods of tax assessment based on units of productivity. Under Diocletian's reforms Egyptians were forced into public service and, to facilitate control, Latin was introduced as the official language, even in provinces where Greek had hitherto been used for official documents. Unification of the Roman Empire was undoubtedly the reason for these reforms, but the Egyptians had had enough. They rebelled so strongly that Diocletian decided that if they could not be subjugated, they should be eliminated. They were dismissed from government service, their property confiscated and their houses levelled. Search was made for Christian literature and copies of the Scriptures, when found, were burned. So harsh is their recollection of the Diocletian era that the Copts adopted a calendar called the Calendar of the Martyrs. The Coptic Calendar begins its era on August 29, 284, in commemoration of those who died for their faith.

Among the earliest recorded martyrs are Saint Sophia, the young daughter of a wealthy Egyptian resident of Memphis, who chose to die rather than make sacrifice before a Roman emperor. Her body was originally buried at Memphis, but was later removed to Constantinople where the famous Cathedral of Saint Sophia was dedicated to her. The holy Damiana, daughter of a governor of the northern Delta, was another martyr. She had retired and found-

38

ed a convent with forty-five women, all of whom were massacred under Diocletian. And Saint Catherine, the daughter of an Alexandrian family, was cruelly tortured when she tried to persuade the Roman emperor Maximianus to convert to Christianity. She was finally beheaded on the emperor's orders, on November 25, 305. Saint Catherine was laid to rest in Alexandria, but later her relics were taken to Sinai where the famous Greek Orthodox monastery bears her name.

It is important to note that the Christian church celebrates both martyrs and confessors. The latter are those who did not suffer the extreme penalty of death. Though hundreds, maybe thousands, died, there was an equal number who escaped, taking their zeal for Christianity with them to create new converts. In a world of want and violence a religion that preached a message of common support and the promise of a blessed life after death was embraced with enthusiasm.

Saint Pachom (Pachomius in Greek, Anba Bakhum in Arabic), an Upper Egyptian who was born about 285, is the founder of a form of monasticism that took his name. He first saw the benefits of unifying the widely-spread Christian communities. Pachom was a native Egyptian who only learned Greek late in life in order to communicate with strangers who came into contact with him. He seems to have been recruited into the Roman army stationed at Thebes. He did not remain in it for long, however, and the reason for his leaving is obscure. A fourth-century Coptic chronicler recorded the fact that he was released from a Roman prison in the year 320, became a professed Christian and was baptised by, and became a disciple of, an aged hermit called Palomen. Palomen was one of the earliest anchorites in the region of Nag Hammadi, and a great spiritual leader in Upper Egypt who was said to have died from excessive fasting. After Pachom had undergone a period of religious training with Palomen, and as a result of a vision, he and a group of followers left the community to establish one of their own, near Akhmim. The caves in the hills flanking the Nile floodplain in Middle Egypt were populated with large numbers of hermits and Pachom slowly drew them together and begin to formulate

39

a rule to govern their daily lives. He introduced a schedule of daily activities for every hour of the day and night: the time to sleep, rise, pray, eat and work. He emphasised that a healthy body provided a healthy spirit and he saw to it that there should be no excesses of any kind, not even spiritual meditation. His aim was to establish a pious, enlightened and self-sufficient community that would set an example to others.

An applicant for admission to Pachom's monastery did not have to exhibit spectacular feats of mortification of the flesh. Although there are numerous examples of physical self-torture in the lives of the Desert Fathers, a candidate for Pachomian monasticism merely had to undergo a period of probation after which he was clothed in the habit of a monk and officially joined the community. The monks were grouped into 'houses' or 'settlements' within the monastery, each according to trade or activity. A supervisor was responsible for each house. The head of the monastery, and spiritual leader of the whole community, was an abbot who ensured that the rules laid down by Pachom were strictly adhered to. No visitors were allowed. When Pachom's sister Mary came to see her brother, she was refused entry to the monastery. Pachom sent a message with the gatekeeper saying: "You have heard that I am living, therefore grieve not that you did not see me. But, if you would renounce the world and find mercy with God, you shall possess your soul. And I trust the Lord to call unto you many who would join you. . . . " Mary, inspired by her brother's words, chose a cave near his monastery and women of similar inclination came to her. Pachom appointed a teacher called Peter for the women, an aged monk noted for his piety and devotion. They were instructed in exactly the same rules as those laid down for men.

The ordered, disciplined community under Pachom's spiritual guidance was so successful that he founded a second, similar institution. It is not without significance that he chose Faw (Pbow), a site due west of Gebel el-Tarif at Nag Hammadi, where a large gnostic community flourished. In other words, the cenobitic (from the Greek 'common' and 'life') movement in Egypt was two-pronged: Egyptian monasteries on the one hand, and gnostic communities on the other. The Egyptian movement represented a microcosm of Egyptian tradition and conservatism, the men being united in their beliefs and in a sense of national identity. The gnostic communities could well be described as a microcosm of the pluralistic society of such cities as Ptolemais, where Egypt's diversified population (Egyptians, Jews, Persians, Macedonians and Greeks) lived and shared beliefs that had merged in a syncretistic alliance. Perhaps Pachom thought to attract some of the more conservative members to his monastery. Be that as it may, Pachom then moved on and established another community, and yet another, until there were no less than eleven Pachomian monasteries in Upper Egypt, including two convents for women.

Pachomian monasticism was made known to the West through the writings of Saint Jerome. He was inspired by the fact that the monks were not endeavouring, through solitary and contemplative devotion, merely to save their own souls. He observed that they encouraged the rural population to come to them for spiritual guidance or healing. Records show that after the death of Pachom there was some dissension and, for a time, expansion of his monastic movement was halted. Shortly thereafter, however, when monasteries and convents were built in great number, some began to follow the rule of Pachom's ideal community instead of their semicenobitic organization.

Saint Pachom translated the Psalms into Coptic around the year 300. The striking similarity between Psalm 104 and Akhenaten's Hymn to the Aten provides another example of the stream of traditional thought and belief between ancient Egypt and Christianity. This is especially remarkable when one realises that Akhenaten's hymn to the Aten was written 1,355 years before the Christian era. Suffice it to present two parallells:

> How manifold is that which thou hast made,
> Hidden from view!
> Thou sole god, there is no other like thee!
> Thou didst create the earth according to thy will,
> being alone. (Akhenaton's Hymn).

41

How manifold are thy works, O Yahweh!
All of them thou hast made by wisdom,
The earth is full of thy creations. (Psalm 104:24)

* * *

When thou dost set in the western horizon,
The earth is in darkness, like to death.
. . . Every lion has come forth from his lair;
All the reptiles bite. (Akhenaten' Hymn)

Thou appointest darkness, that it may be night,
In which all the beasts of the forest prowl:
The young lions roaring for their prey,
To seek their food from God. (Psalm 104:20 ff).

The famous revelation of the emperor Constantine in 312, which resulted in his conversion to Christianity, was followed by the Edict of Milan according to which the principle of religious tolerance was established throughout the Roman empire. It was at last safe to admit to being a Christian in Egypt and out of the catacombs and caves came many monks and hermits to build churches and monasteries.

The theological disputes that had plagued the early Christian movement became even more fierce in the fourth and following centuries. The controversies, as already mentioned, centred on the attempt to define the Incarnation: if Jesus was both God and Man, had He two natures? If so, what was their relationship? The chief protagonists were the Arians, so called after Arius, the elderly Alexandrian presbyter, and the Monophysites under the bishop Alexander. The former held that "a time there was when He was not." In other words, that Jesus did not have the same nature as the Father. The Monophysites regarded this as recognition of two gods and a reversion to polytheism. They believed that Father and Son were one nature; that Jesus was both divine and human.

Considering the abstract nature of the dispute, it was discussed

42

in an atmosphere both highly charged and antagonistic. In fact, it reached such an impasse that a need was felt to define officially a dogma to unify Christian belief. The Council of Nicea, on the shores of the Black Sea, was convened in 325 for this purpose. It was the earliest and most important church council, the first meeting between the Church and the State. It was attended by the emperor Constantine and three hundred and eighteen bishops and their delegations from Egypt, Syria, Assyria, Asia Minor, Greece and the West.

The Syrian and Assyrian delegations included bishops from Antioch, Jerusalem and Armenia. Goths and Romans represented the West. The Alexandrian delegation included the bishop Alexander and his deacon, Athanasius, Arius his antagonist, and a large body of monks and hermits, many of whom bore disfigurements from Roman persecution. Both Potamon ('dedicated to Amon') the bishop of Heracleopolis Magna (Ehnasia), and Paphnutius ('dedicated to his god'), from the Theban area, had a right eye gouged out with a sword and the empty socket seared with a red-hot poker.

The deputation from Egypt, which had raised the question which the council was to decide, was the most argumentative of the representatives. In fact, the meeting started in dignity and solemnity but ended in an atmosphere of exasperation and antipathy. Each of the representatives was committed to his opinion and hostile to the that of other nations. From the moment the debate started, accusations were levelled and bandied around. The anger was, perhaps, not surprising in view of the fact that the council was held to settle questions that had already violently divided the church. It was the consequence, not the cause of, religious dissension and there were personal jealousies and grievances. The tall, dazzlingly attired emperor Constantine must have been sadly disillusioned with the Christian world torn by factions.

The leading sees attending the council were Alexandria and Antioch, the former represented by the bishop Eusebius and the latter by the bishop Alexander. Although Alexander officially led Egypt's delegation it was his deacon, Athanasius, who was his chief spokesman. And it says a great deal for the eloquence, reasoning

43

and persistence of Alexander's young deacon that the Nicene creed, to the effect that Father and Son are of the same nature, was sanctioned:

> We believe in one God, the Father all-Sovereign, maker of all things, both visible and invisible: And in one Lord Jesus Christ, the Son of God, begotten of the Father, an only-begotten; that is, from the essence of the Father, God from God, Light from Light, true God from true God—begotten, not made—being of one essence with the Father; by whom all things were made, both things in heaven and things on earth; who for us men and for our salvation came down and was made flesh, was made man, suffered, and rose again the third day, ascended into heaven, cometh to judge the quick and the dead: And in the Holy Spirit. (Translation from Gwatkin, H.M., in *The Cambridge Medieval History*, Vol. I, pp. 121–22).

Constantine formally received the decision of the bishops and issued a decree of banishment against those who refused to subscribe to it. Arius was denounced as a heretic and his books were burned.

The bishop Alexander and his deacon Athanasius returned to Egypt triumphant. The former had emerged from the Arian controversy as the Orthodox Patriarch of Alexandria and a universally accepted doctor of the Christian Church. Moreover, the monastic orders were stamped with ecclesiastical approval at the Council of Nicea. When Alexander died soon afterwards, Athanasius succeeded to the vacant see. He had the Egyptian nation behind him and the respect of the Christian world before him.

Athanasius (312–372), the remarkable representative of the church of Egypt, is *the only theologian whose fame is common to both East and West*. For this reason, and also because the Nicene creed still retains a hold on the mass of Christendom (it had a place in all

Western liturgies at least until the end of the seventeenth century), let us take a look at the man who fought for it.

The historical appearance of Athanasius is well documented. Alexander, the bishop of Alexandria, was entertaining the clergy in his home overlooking the sea-front while a group of children were playing on the shore. They seemed to be enacting a religious cere-mony, so Alexander sent for them and asked what game they were playing. They finally admitted that they had been imitating the sacrament of baptism. The one boy, Athanasius, who had enacted the role of bishop, recited all the proper questions and rituals he had performed; when Alexander realised that he had left none out in his addresses, and had dipped the boys in the sea, he declared that the baptism was valid and he personally confirmed them. It was then that the bishop took Athanasius under his charge and later made him deacon.

The ethnic origin of Athanasius is not clear. The fact that he was bilingual indicates Egyptian ancestry because the Greeks seldom bothered to learn the native tongue. Although his name is Greek, it was, as already noted, common practise for educated Egyptians to adopt or give their sons Greek names, just as they adopted Greek names for their cities and their gods and goddesses. Athanasius was small in stature, wore a short beard and had light auburn hair, which is a characteristic found on many Egyptian mummies. Al-though this description might be compatible with pure Egyptian des-cent, the argument is inconclusive. More persuasive, perhaps, is the fact that Athanasius spoke the Egyptian vernacular, sympathised with Egyptian sentiments, understood the Egyptian people, and was ardently nationalistic. He became a hermit in his early life. He was a close friend and biographer of Saint Antony with whom he com-municated in the Egyptian language, since Antony was not bi-lingual. Later, when Athanasius was driven into exile during the theological disputes that were to split the church, he sought refuge among the Desert Fathers. But those events yet lay in the future.

Soon after the Council of Nicea and the success of the Alexan-drian delegation, the bishop of Antioch founded a school in imitation of that of Alexandria. Then, three years later the emperor Constantine founded a new capital. He chose the ancient Greek town of Byzantium, which became Constantinople (Constantine's city). It was the first Christian city and it was to gain the importance and prestige that had once belonged to Alexandria. It was embellished with great monuments that were shipped there from many ancient cities, including an obelisk over thirty metres high transported from Egypt. Constantinople, known as New Rome, became a new metropolis of Greek art and science as well as a refuge of Christian and secular learning. It undermined the reputation Alexandria had held as the seat of learning since Ptolemaic times.

The see of Alexandria faced another setback when the Arian leaders were recalled from banishment at the entreaty of Princess Constantia. Constantine's successor, Constantius, also favoured the Arians. He deposed Athanasius, set his followers to flee at the point of the sword, and placed his own bishop, Georgius, on the throne of the see of Alexandria. Thus began an era when ecclesiastical dignitaries excommunicated one another, and mobs sacked churches of opposing factions. Athanasius was driven into exile five times and sought shelter with hermits in their isolated caves. He lived with Saint Antony near the Red Sea, and he also lived in the monastery in Kharga Oasis for many years. During his exiles, Athanasius successfully reconciled the differences between monks and the hermits, some of whom did not want to join the monastic order, preferring their own semi-cenobitic communities.

Political unrest continued. Under Theodosius I (375–395) Christianity was formally declared the religion of the empire, and the Arians were again declared heathens. The Monophysites were reinstated, but their power was limited as a result of the partition of the empire between the emperor Honorius of Rome and the emperor Arcadius of Constantinople. Egypt fell under the jurisdiction of the latter. Theophilus was made Patriarch of Alexandria and he displayed tremendous zeal in destroying heathen temples. A wave of destruction swept over the land of Egypt. Tombs were ravished, walls of ancient monuments scraped and statues toppled. The famous statue of Serapis was burned and the Serapium in Alexandria de-

46

stroyed, along with its library of an estimated 42,800 books. It was a folly of fanaticism in the name of orthodoxy not, ironically, so different from that which had earlier oppressed Christianity in Rome.

The whole of the New Testament was translated into Coptic at this time (only the Psalms and selected writings had been translated before). The translators used a more colloquial form of their language than that used by demotic scribes, thus making their writings — biblical, theological and liturgical — available to many more Egyptians. They also chose the Egyptian word *neter* to describe God; it survived in Coptic as *nute*. But the specific meaning of the word, both its original in hieroglyphics, and its derivative, has been lost. Generations of scholars have deliberated over the actual meaning of the word and are, even today, not in agreement on its definition. Suffice it to say that the ancient Egyptians used both the singular *neter* and the plural *neteru*, side by side in their mortuary texts. And that the Copts chose the former word because, presumably, there was no other that so aptly conveyed to their minds the conception of an active force — commanding, guiding, inspiring and ordaining man's destiny.

Many ancient temples were converted into monastic centers in the fourth and fifth centuries: Deir (monastery) el-Medina and Deir el-Bahri on the Theban necropolis are two well-known examples. Churches were built in great number inside the chambers of ancient temples. For example, in the second court of the mortuary temple of Ramses III at Medinet Habu, and the Court of Amenhotep III in Luxor Temple. One of the earliest Christian buildings in Egypt was constructed between the birth-house and the coronation-house of the Temple of Hathor at Dendera. Some of the blocks from the birth-house were, in fact, reused in the church's construction. It is possible that this church marked the famous Christian centre of the fourth century, for Saint Jerome described an assembly of fifty thousand monks who celebrated Easter somewhere in the neighbourhood of Dendera.

Pilgrims came from all over the Christian world to visit the monasteries in Egypt. Rufinus, 380–401, in his ecclesiastical history, described a meeting of ten thousand monks at Arsinoë (ancient Crocodilopolis) in the Fayoum. This figure was repeated by Palladius, a fourth-century poet; in his *Historia Lausiaca* he added that there were also twelve convents for women at Arsinoë. The bishop of Bahnasa estimated the number of monks in Middle Egypt at ten thousand, and nuns at twenty thousand, living in forty monasteries and convents. Archaeological evidence has revealed a huge monastic settlement in distant Kharga Oasis, in the western desert, dating from the fourth century. Its necropolis of Bagawat contains over two hundred chapels. Wadi Natrun once had fifty monasteries and over five thousand monks. East of Wadi Natrun, at Kelya (Latin for 'cell'), there are about seven hundred and fifty abandoned hermitages dating to around the fifth century. This site was described in many early Christian writings, such as those of Palladius and Rufinus. In the biography of Saint Macrufius, who lived in the sixth century, the village of Ishnin al-Nasarah is reported to have had "as many churches as there were days in the year," and he described two thousand youths wearing the cowl, a thousand of them "virginal monks," apart from the old men and the old women who had married and had then renounced the world.

As with most great movements that spread beyond the borders of the country in which they took root, contradictory traditions of the origins of monasticism have emerged. Western tradition credits Saint Paul, who lived around the middle of the third century, with being the first hermit, largely as a result of his *Life*, written by Saint Jerome in the fourth century. Copts, however, do not regard his ascetic ideal as atypical of the period in which he lived. Saint Antony, whose fame spread as a result of his biography written after his death by Athanasius around 250, holds a more prominent position in Egyptian tradition as founder of the monastic movement and the prototype of the Egyptian monk. One of his disciples, Makar, stayed with him on at least two occasions and later established Antonian monasticism in the desert of Scetis, west of the Delta.

The Christian ideal could, therefore, be said to have been acted out in different modes of behaviour throughout Egypt, from the ordinary Christian layman to the solitary recluse, from the urban priest to the cloistered nun, from sprawling monastic communities like those of Wadi Natrun and Bagawat to the walled Pachomian monasteries.

And still factional disputes continued, especially when the see of Alexandria lost precedence to the see of Constantinople at the Council of Constantinople in 381. There were riots and the Catechetical School, which had remained a force in the intellectual life of Alexandria for nearly two centuries, was destroyed. The rift had become a question of Egypt's political opposition to the the the Melkites, or emperor's men, representing the Eastern church. In other words, when Constantinople was heretical under the Arian emperor Constantius, Egypt was orthodox. When Constantinople was orthodox, Egypt broke away and founded its own national Coptic Church.

The Council of Chalcedon in 451 was convened in a final effort to unify the Christian world. In fact, it eventually led to the schism that alienated Egypt from both the Eastern and the Western (Latin) churches forever. Although the creed of the earlier Council of Nicea, formulated by Athanasius, was left largely unchanged, some minor adjustments were made: an additional clause opened the way to the possibility of future additions, and the phrase that defined 'begotten of the Father' was dropped. The Nicene creed in its revised form was accepted by the Eastern Churches but the Egyptian Monophysites strongly resisted any change whatsoever. They would not compromise. The fact that the precedence of the see of Constantinople, over the see of Alexandria, was ratified at the Council of Chalcedon undoubtedly had something to do with the stubborn refusal of the Egyptian nationalists to accept any modification.

The Monophysites clung to Athanasius' original doctrine and their strength grew. The Eastern church of Constantinople, with its Greek adherents in Alexandria, gradually weakened under local pressure. By the reign of Justinian (527–565) the Monophysites far outnumbered the opposing Melkite party in Egypt and refused to be coerced by them. Justinian tried drastic measures, imprisoning

49

Monophysites in the fortress of Babylon, but all this succeeded in doing was to aggravate the differences. The Egyptian church formally separated from the Eastern Roman Church. Forthwith the Egyptian Christians, the Copts, appointed their own patriarch of Alexandria and followed their own interpretation of Scriptures, while the Eastern Church, the Melkites, did the same. They also consecrated a patriarch in Alexandria. To this day there are two lines of patriarchs, one Monophysite (Coptic) and one Melkite (Greek Orthodox).

In the fifth and sixth centuries when both the Eastern Church of Constantinople (with their Greek adherents in Alexandria) and the Western church of Rome, basked in the glory of imperial favour, accumulated great endowments, built splendid churches and elaborated the ceremonial of worship, the Coptic clergy had to stint to survive. The Roman church began to turn increasingly to Antioch and Palestine for an ascetic ideal, and Egypt's great contribution to the Christian world was dismissed as a heresy.

Nevertheless, the Copts regard theirs as the orthodox Church that held firm to the Nicene creed, as formulated in the first and greatest of the church councils. They take pride in the fact that Antony, an Egyptian hermit, remains the spiritual father of Christianity, and that Athanasius, his disciple, was its first spokesman in the West. All Christian monasticism stems, either directly or indirectly, from the Egyptian example: Saint Basil, organiser of the monastic movement in Asia Minor, visited Egypt around 357 and his rule is followed by the Eastern Churches; Saint Jerome, who translated the Bible into Latin, came to Egypt around 400 and left details of his experiences in his letters; Saint Benedict founded monasteries in the sixth century on the model of Saint Pachom, but in a stricter form. And countless pilgrims visited the Desert Fathers and emulated their spiritual, disciplined lives. There is even indication, but no conclusive evidence, of a Coptic missionary movement as far afield as Ireland, since Irish monasticism is closer to Saint Pachom than Saint Benedict. The Ethiopian church is an offshoot of the Coptic church; its bishop was consecrated by Athanasius in the fourth century. The Nubian church was the result of Egyptian missionary work.

It is interesting to observe that on the Coptic patriarch of Alexandria fell the responsibility of determining the exact day for the celebration of each successive Easter, and of announcing it for each following year by special messengers, sent immediately after the Feast of Epiphany, to all the towns and monasteries within their jurisdiction, including the Western church through the bishop of Rome, and the Syrian church through the bishop of Antioch. The Coptic Church, a remarkable monument of Christian antiquity, looks back with great pride to the age when its authority was acknowledged by all Christian sees. It recites the original Nicene creed formulated by Athanasius, which has a place also in the liturgies and confessions of the western church through the church of Rome.

Arab Conquest of Egypt. When Egypt was conquered by the Arabs in AD 641 the Melkite patriarch went back to Constantinople and a Greek Orthodox patriarch was elected in Alexandria, which had become no more than a provincial backwater. The Arab conquerors chose Egypt's ancient capital of Memphis as venue for their discussions with the Egyptians, the *Gibt*, from which Copt is derived.

The conversion of the bulk of the Egyptian population to the Muslim faith was slow. In the seventh century the Copts were taxed as protected non-Muslims and seem to have enjoyed some prosperity. In the Abbasid Dynasties, from 750 to 868 and from 905 to 935, sumptuary laws were imposed them, but during the Fatimid period (969–1171) the Coptic Church generally flourished. Surviving literature from monastic centres dates largely from the eighth to the tenth centuries. There was no drastic break in the activities of Coptic craftsmen, such as weavers, leather-binders and wood-workers. By the eleventh century there were bi-lingual Coptic-Arabic liturgical manuscripts. Only when Saladin founded the Ayyubid dynasty in the twelvth century did the conflict between Middle Eastern and European states sharpen. During the Crusades the Christian community in Egypt shrank to a minority.

Inside the Monastery of St. Paul, Red Sea. Photograph by Cassandra Vivian.

Street decoration in Old Cairo. Photograph by Robert Scott.

2

COPTIC CHRISTIANITY TODAY

The Copts, Orthodox Egyptian Christians, though a minority within a Muslim country, number some seven million people. Apart from Cairo and the Delta city of Tanta, they are most strongly represented in Middle and Upper Egypt: Assiut, Akhmim, Girgeh, Nagada, Kuft, Luxor, Esna and Dendera. There are one hundred and fifty Coptic organisations in Cairo alone, including schools, orphanages, old age homes, hospitals, and social service centres. The spiritual leader of the Coptic community is Pope Shenuda III who was released from 'house arrest' in 1983 by President Mubarak. The pope had been ordered into detention by the late President Sadat, along with eight bishops and twenty-two priests, accused of emphasising Coptic identity to the extent of fomenting unrest and generally encouraging hostility to the government.

The Coptic language, the direct line of communication with the past, has been lost as a living language. Today the ritual chanted in Coptic services, the prayers and the mass, may be the language of the pharaohs but it is understood by neither the priests nor the people. Consequently, after reciting the gospel in Coptic it is rendered into vernacular Arabic. Although the dialect used in present-day church liturgies is *Bohairic*, which was adopted when the Monastery of Saint Makar (Macarius) in Wadi Natrun became the official residence of the patriarch, linguists have observed that the language contained ancient local dialects, including *Sahidic* in Upper Egypt, *Fayumic* in the area of the Fayoum, *Akhmimic* around Akhmim and the closely related "Middle Egyptian" dialect. The Coptic language was gradually replaced by Arabic after the Arab conquest of Egypt in 640. Yet, its extinction was so slow that even in the fifteenth century al-Makrizi implied that it was still used. Today it survives only in some vernacular Arabic names, specifically the names of the Coptic months, which are derived from the names of ancient Egyptian gods; *Tut*, for example, derived from Thoth, and *Hatur* from Hathor. Although urban Copts pride themselves on being the only true descendents of the ancient Egyptians, this is no less true for the rural population of Egypt, both Muslim and Christian, who have preserved their character, customs and traditions.

Coptic music is vocal music and hymns were composed in the style of popular songs. There is no trace of musical notation in these hymns. Demetrius of Phalaron, the librarian in Alexandria in 297 BC, told of ceremonies in honour of Egyptian gods using seven Greek vowels, one by one, thus producing harmonious sounds and eliminating the need for instrumental accompaniment. These sounds, wrote Nichomachus, a mathematician who lived about AD 100, are the vowels of seven stars; to this day these same seven vowels are chanted in Coptic hymns.

Seven being a sacred number, Copts observe seven canonical sacraments: baptism, confirmation, eucharist, penance, orders, matrimony and unction of the sick. In the Coptic church, a child is usually baptised within a week or two of birth and is plunged wholly under water three times. Confirmation is simultaneous with the act of baptism. In common with the Roman Catholic practice, the Copts require that the water be specially consecrated. Copts continue to be circumcised following ancient Egyptian traditions.

In church services the members of the congregation are separated by sex, males to the left and females to the right. The latter are not obliged to cover their heads but they may not, under any circumstances, enter the sanctuary behind the screen. Men, if they do so, observe the custom of first removing their shoes before stepping on the holy ground around the altar. On entering a church all members of the congregation cross themselves, kneel before the altar and pay homage to the pictures of saints and the Holy Virgin on the walls.

A sense of awe and mysticism surrounds the sacerdotal functions in a Coptic church, which largely take place in the holy inner chambers out of sight of the congregation. Apart from eucharistic vessels, the Copts use five basic instruments: the chalice, a ritual goblet with a small conical bowl, which is almost straight-sided, with a long stem ending in a round knob and a circular foot; the paten, which is a flat, circular dish without a depression in the middle but with a vertical raised rim; the dome, which is placed over the consecrated bread in the middle of the paten; the spoon for administering communion (in Coptic tradition it is the custom to put the wafer in the wine and administer both together), and the altar-casket, a small cubical box, the top of which has a circular opening large enough to admit the chalice. Incense has, from ancient times, been regarded as important to help create a desirable atmosphere of spirituality and it remains so in Coptic churches today. There is a reverence for sacred acts performed by children, especially young boys spreading incense, usually from metal censers. When not conducting a service, the priest comes among the people and they kiss his hand while he blesses them. Coptic Orthodox priests have the right to marry, but the high clergy do not.

Egyptians are extremely pious people. Copts frequently have religious pictures in their houses and pray before them or burn tapers beside them as offerings in fulfilment of a vow. Although the worship of saints is expressly forbidden by the church, a visit to Old Cairo will reveal many a faithful Christian touching or honouring pictures, especially Saint Michael, the Holy Virgin, Saint George and Saint Makar. Among the feasts or birthdays of the saints in the Coptic calendar, the days on which they were martyred are regarded as holy days.

Coptic weddings, which do not take place during the season of Lent, are surrounded by solemnity and ritual during the church service and there is a splendid celebration afterwards. The betrothed couple, who may be as closely related as second cousins, are first formally engaged and the bride-to-be receives an engagement ring. Sometimes the family have a small church service to bless the occasion and the engagement usually lasts for about a year. During this time the couple gets to know one another (especially if the union has been arranged between the two families) and the dowry and the furnishings for their home are discussed by their respective families.

On the day of the wedding, the bride and the bridegroom are escorted separately to the church. The bride wears a white wedding dress and veil and the church is decorated with candles, flowers and sometimes ribbons connecting the benches of the congregation. The service lasts for an hour, or more, amidst incense burning and the sound of bells and tambourines. Crowns are briefly placed on the heads of the wedded couple before they leave the church. The reception is usually a lavish affair at a private club or hotel and then the couple either leave for a honeymoon or move directly into their new, fully-furnished home. A church service is not compulsory; a couple may be married by a priest in their own home. But it is the duty of the priest to make sure that both parties are acting of their own free will. Village weddings are similar but are naturally more modest. After the church service the bride's furniture is ceremoniously transported to their new home.

It is extremely difficult to obtain a Coptic divorce. The procedure is long and complicated and only granted in extreme circumstances, such as adultery (proved according to the civil law), neglect of children or, in the event a man becomes a Muslim in order to marry another woman, his wife may sue for divorce on grounds of bigamy.

It would require a separate volume to enumerate the religious customs of a people so much given to ceremony as the Copts. The most important celebrations are Palm Sunday and Holy Week leading to Easter, a holiday more important even than Christmas. The celebration begins with a solemn midnight mass on the Sunday before Easter, at which the priest or bishop blesses branches of the palm tree. A procession then forms with the clergy bearing crosses, incense tapers and palm branches. They sing and move to each altar, the principal pictures, and the reliquaries, starting the week of prayer. Copts carry palm branches to graveyards and weave baskets and crosses from palm fronds. The feast of Epiphany is another great celebration. It consists of benediction of water for the whole community performed by the bishop or patriarch in full pontifical apparel.

The Coptic Christmas is on the 7th of January and *Laila Kabir*,

57

the Big Night, is on the 6th. It ends fifteen days of fasting, when no animal food is taken. A large meal is eaten at sundown followed by a church service and midnight mass. Early on Christmas morning children go to church in new, brightly coloured clothes, to light a candle and receive a blessing. For adults there is an exchange of visits. Most of the women stay at home throughout the day to welcome visitors, while the men schedule part of their time to pay visits, themselves, to the homes of relatives and neighbours. It is a day for sharing and spreading goodwill. During the last ten years Western Christmas tradition has taken root in Egypt. This is not to say that the Copts celebrate their own Christmas any differently, but merely that in December Christmas trees and baubles are sold; Western Christmas Eve, on December 24th is now celebrated in Egypt much as New Year's Eve festivities are in the West. December 25th, however, is not a public holiday.

The Copts have seasons of fasting matched by no other Christian community. These include a pre-Lent fast of two weeks that is observed a month before Lent begins. This is known as the Great Fast, which begins on the day after the feast of the Epiphany, on Monday, and continues for forty days until Palm Sunday during which time no meat, eggs or fish are consumed, and it is forbidden to drink wine or coffee. Moreover, no food or drink whatsoever may be taken between sunrise and sunset. The Muslim Ramadan closely resembles the Coptic Lent in its strict regulations as well as the granting of a dispensation for illness or weakness. The third great Coptic observance is the Fast of the Apostles, which also lasts for forty days, after Ascension. There is, in addition, the fast in honour of the Assumption of the Virgin for fifteen days from the first day of August, and the Fast of the Nativity for twenty-eight days before Christmas.

Among the Egyptians a sense of the supernatural was, and remains, extremely strong. They believe in both miracles and magic: miracles like visitations of the Holy Virgin, whose last appearance was in Old Cairo in 1973; and magic like the belief in the efficacy of sacred charms. Egyptians also believe in the Evil Eye—that the casting of a covetous look causes grievous harm—and they entreat holy men, priests or Muslim sheikhs, to exorcise on their behalf. They visit the tombs of saints and martyrs on holy days and at Easter, joyously confident that their celebration of the "second birth" of the saint to a life everlasting will bring blessings on them. The belief in the power of patron saints is extremely strong in Egypt. If, among the poor, prayers to God are of no avail, both Christians and Muslims ask a scribe to write a letter to a specific saint with pleas as varied as curing the sick to solving personal problems. These letters are not signed because, as in ancient times when letters were written by scribes addressed to the dead or to local deities, it is taken for granted that the holy saint knows who has written them. Since ancient times, Egyptians have worn sacred charms, amulets or talismans for protection.

It is interesting to note that Egyptians still observe some traditions that appear to have their origins in the remote past. For example, there is the fortieth-day observance for the release of the soul from the body that might be related to the fact that it took a minimum of forty days (and up to seventy days) for the mummification of the deceased in ancient times. That is to say, there is a similar period of mourning. When Egyptians place flowers at the graves of the dead in annual remembrance and on important religious holidays, food is also taken and eaten there; in ancient times food and drink that were placed on an offering table for the *ka*, or spirit of the deceased, was regarded as specially blessed, and was eaten.

Reverence for the Holy Family is widespread in Egypt and there is a strong and persistent tradition that supports the Bible story (Matt. 2:13-15) of the Flight into Egypt. Literally dozens of sites throughout the Delta and Middle Egypt enjoy a tradition of the Holy Family having visited, rested or taken refreshment there during the sojourn to Egypt. Many towns have a *mulid* or annual festival in honour of the Virgin, which is celebrated by Christians and Muslims alike. In the Koran, the Muslim Holy Book, Jesus is regarded as a prophet along with Abraham, Moses and Mohammed, and Myriam, the Mother of Jesus of Nazareth, is also venerated.

One of the great celebrations that is shared by Copts and Muslims is the annual pilgrimage to Gebel al-Tair (Mount of Birds), almost opposite Samalut in Middle Egypt. This was the site where Mary, according to tradition, feared for the safety of Jesus because a large rock threatened to fall on their boat from the mountain overlooking the river. But Jesus extended His hand and prevented its falling. His imprint remained on the rock and the Church of the Lady of the Palm was built in commemoration of the visit.

The pilgrimage at Gebel al-Tair starts on the western bank of the Nile. Young and old, rich and poor, travel from neighbouring villages and, indeed, from distant provinces. They come by train, by donkey-cart or on foot. Children are clad in gaily coloured clothes, often with bright head-scarves. They cross the river from Samalut to the eastern bank of the Nile on river craft assembled for the occasion and then they join a convoy of vehicles of all kinds, filled with happy, laughing people, clapping, drumming and singing. They travel from the banks of the Nile to the foot of the mountain where the pilgrims unload bedding, baskets of food and even cooking equipment and then they start to climb. Such a pilgrimage is no short homage. Egyptians have come from distant provinces for an extended visit.

At the top of Gebel al-Tair is the church dedicated to the Holy Virgin. Outside its walls the people stake their territory, laying down mattresses, personal belongings and provisions. Vendors appear with baskets of paper hats and whistles for the children. Each day the pilgrims enter the church, pass their hands across paintings of Mary and Jesus and move their lips in silent prayer. The site enjoys great popularity because it is believed to have healing qualities.

In view of the fact that there is no historical evidence to support the story of Jesus' sojourn in Egypt (there is silence by the four evangelists between His youth and the beginning of His public ministry), the popularity of such a pilgrimage points to its possible association with an older tradition. What comes to mind is the similarity between the Virgin Mother and the mother goddess of ancient Egypt, Isis. Mary, like Isis, hid her Son from those who would do Him harm and, like the ancient goddess, has become associated with the powers of healing in Egypt.

Coptic and Koranic sources are not always in agreement on the route that was taken by the Holy Family nor on the length of their stay in Egypt. The Coptic Church claims it to have been for a little over three and a half years. Muslims believe that the Holy Family stayed in Egypt for seven years and that Jesus went to school in Middle Egypt. The differing traditions concerning specific places are interesting to note. For example, east of Bahnasa, near Beni Mazar, is the site of the ancient city of Oxyrhynchus, which was an episcopal see in the fifth century. Today it is predominently Muslim. The local sheikhs claim that a passage (XXIII: 50) of the Koran refers to Bahnasa: " . . . and we have made the Son of Mary and His Mother a portent, and we gave them refuge on a height, a place of flocks and water-springs," and further, that Jesus attended school there when He was nine years old. They quote the Muslim historian Mohammed al-Bakir (676–731) as their source and explain that when the teacher asked Jesus to say the alphabet, He did not recite it, but explained it thus: "The *alif* stands for the good deeds of God, the *da* for His glory, the *geem* for His splendour . . . the *ka* is the Word of God that will never change . . . " and so on. Coptic priests in Bahnasa, on the other hand, maintain that the Holy Family remained in hiding for four days only and that they took refuge beside the canal Bahr Youssef (Joseph's canal).

Among the numerous sites that enjoy popularity as places where the Holy Family rested are the towns of Bubastis (Tell Basta), Bilbais, Samanud and Sakha in the Delta, where annual pilgrimages are made. Also the area of Wadi Natrun, west of the Delta, which is one of the most famous monastic sites in Egypt. The area of Babylon (Old Cairo) and Mataria (Heliopolis), are also hallowed sites. The latter enjoys popularity as the place where the Blessed Virgin rested beneath a tree, refreshed herself and washed the clothes of the Child in the spring. (What is today known as the "Tree of the Virgin" at Mataria grew from the shoot of a sycamore that was planted in 1672 and fell on June 14, 1906. According to a medieval Arab writer the original tree was a balsam.) The Church of the Holy Virgin on the banks of the Nile at Maadi, a suburb south of Cairo, is believed to be the site where the Holy Family embarked by boat for Upper Egypt. Sites where celebrations in honour of the visit are regularly made are Bahnasa, Kais, Gebel al-Tair, Ashmounein (near Mallawi), Phyls and (according to Coptic sources only) Assiut, where the Holy Family stayed in a mountain range in ancient rock-tombs. Biblical, Coptic and Koranic traditions are in agreement that the Holy Family left the fertile Nile valley at Qusia (Qusqam of the Bible) and travelled south-west towards Meir and al- Muharrak. There the Holy Family hid in a cave while Joseph built a small house of bricks and covered it with palm leaves. At al-Muharrak an angel of the Lord appeared to Joseph in a dream and said, "Arise and take the young child and His Mother, and go into the land of Israel for they are dead which sought the young child's life." (Matt. 2:20.).

Pilgrimages to shrines and holy places were a central part of Egypt's religious practice from pharaonic times and even in late antiquity people went to pray at the tombs of saints or martyrs where their bodies or relics were housed and where a saintly "presence" was felt. Copts are not alone in finding it easier to have an actual object of religious identification as a focal point of worship, rather then abstract dogma. In villages throughout the Nile valley people claim to possess a relic (or relics) of a saint or martyr and have built shrines to house them. If it is a relic of a well-known saint, especially the head, this is particularly important. The head of Saint Mark the Evangelist, for example, is a relic so holy that it has been variously described in medieval and modern texts as being in Alexandria, Venice, Wadi Natrun and the Cathedral of Saint Mark in Cairo. The body of Saint George, on the other hand—according to Coptic and Abyssinian traditions—is buried without a head. Saint George was a Roman legionary who defied Diocletian and was martyred in Asia. His body was said to have been brought to Egypt by the Coptic Partriarch Gabriel II in the twelfth century. On the day that the Copts celebrate his martrydom, the body of Saint George is brought out of the shrine at the oasis of al-Bahnasa (which the late Egyptologist Ahmed Fakhry identified with Bahriyah Oasis), a new veil is put over it and it is carried in procession all over the town. The old veil is cut to pieces and these are kept as sacred relics.

Devotion to patron saints through their relics has continued through the ages. Copts pray before the chamber housing them and leave candles or pieces of cloth attached to the railing or screen in front of them. Relics are also transferred from one area to another. In the Monastery of Saint Makar in Wadi Natrun, the monks move from the church of Saint Makar to the Church of the Forty-Nine Martyrs during the winter; whenever the divine liturgy is celebrated, it is in the presence of the saints — the three Macarii and John the Little — whose relics are carried by the monks.

Both the sanctifying of revered people and the transference of parts of their bodies from site to site are also part of an ancient pattern of ritual in the Nile valley that lingered on in the new Christian setting. The former is reminiscent of each province in ancient Egypt claiming possession of part of the sacred body of the legendary ancestor Osiris, who was slain by his wicked brother Set, and erecting shrines in his honour. Great importance was attached to the head of Osiris, which was said to be buried in the sacred city of Abydos, but it was also claimed that it lay at other sites as well. As for the transference of revered objects this, too, has its parallel in ancient Egypt: festivals like the annual *Feast of Opet* in Luxor when the sacred statue of the god Amon was borne in splendid procession from Luxor temple to Karnak at the height of the flood, is one example. The great New Year Festival of Horus at Edfu, when the statue of the goddess Hathor was taken from Dendera to Edfu, is another.

A tradition does not die if it is meaningful to a community, although it may undergo considerable change with the passage of time. Christianity took hold in Egypt because it shared the same characteristics as the mystery cults, especially in the central mystery, the resurrection of the body and the afterlife. Egyptians embraced Christianity because it gave them familiar altars, priesthoods, a heavenly hierarchy of angels, and God as the father and fashioner of order. The doctrine of future rewards and punishments had its

63

origins in the distant past, in the Negative Confession before Osiris. The efficacy of prayer, forgiveness of sins, and the rite of baptism or purification with water, existed in Egypt for thousands of years before the Christian era. It is interesting to note that the Coptic church is the only church that confers ordination, not by imposition of hands but by the act of breathing, which seems also to be an ancient tradition. The expression "giving the breath of life" is a common one in Egyptian texts. The revealed Christian truth is different from ancient practices in its exclusive worship of one God.

Copts are avidly interested in their heritage. Many young people spend their weekends in the churches of Old Cairo volunteering their expertise to interested visitors. They are not tourist guides but genuine, pious youths who are proud of their heritage. Copts are also eager to learn of new discoveries that might shed more light on the early Christian period. One of the most important finds this century was a codex containing the Book of Proverbs in its entirety, dating to the fifth century. The manuscript, written in the *Sahidic* dialect, was found in the hills of Old Cairo and published by the University of Egypt in 1927. In December 1984 the daily Arabic newspaper *Al Ahram* carried the announcement of "the most important Coptic document to be found since the Nag Hammadi codices." This was the oldest *complete* manuscript of the psalms of David, written in Coptic in the 'middle Egyptian' dialect, and it was found on the outskirts of Beni Suef. The text, which had been placed in an undecorated wooden box below the head of a mummified child, has been sent for conservation prior to study.

The new Cathedral of Saint Mark off Ramses Street in Cairo is the pride of the Coptic community. It has a seating capacity of five thousand people and the Patriarchal Library is located there. The Cathedral was founded in 1965, on the occasion of the 1900th anniversary of the martyrdom of Saint Mark and the transportation of his relics from Venice to Cairo. The relics originally reposed in the Church of Saint Mark in Alexandria but around the year 828 two merchants removed the body to Venice where the famous Cathedral of Saint Mark was erected in 883. According to tradition the head of the evangelist remained in Egypt, variously described as being carried to Wadi Natrun, Cairo and Alexandria, respectively. Copts claim that today it is in an ebony box in the crypt beneath the altar of the Cathedral of Saint Mark in Alexandria, which was reconstructed in 1952.

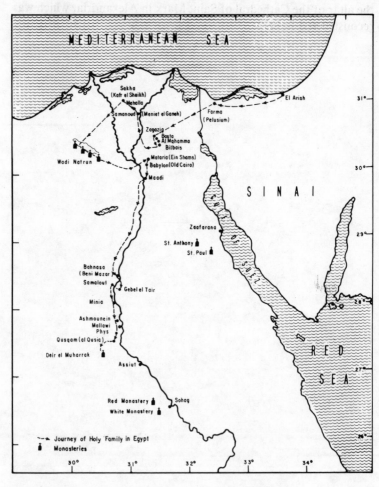

Map of Egypt showing the Flight of the Holy Family

Christ enthroned. Detail of painted niche from Bawit Monastery. Now in the Coptic Museum. Photograph by Robert Scott.

67

3

COPTIC ART

Coptic art, the distinctive Christian art of Egypt, includes works of a diverse character because there was no separation between "art" and "craft" in the early Christian era; the capital of a column or an illustrated manuscript were as much forms of creative expression as paintings and sculpture. From burial grounds, there are objects like funerary stelae, or tombstones, *cartonnage* sarcophagi and fragments of woven textiles from clothing in which the deceased were laid to rest. Monastic centres, churches and shrines provide stone and wood-carvings, metalwork, wall and panel-paintings, as well as a wealth of utilitarian objects like ivory combs, wooden seals for impressing sacred bread, pottery and glassware.

Coptic art owes a great debt to two main sources: the classical world and ancient Egypt. Objects made in Greek style, or under the direct influence of classical art, include stone carvings of winged victories or cupids bearing garlands, the vine branches of Bacchus, Aphrodite, Leda, and Hercules. Monuments of mixed Greek-Egyptian character are relief slabs that were probably used as wall decorations in churches; they frequently feature pilasters surmounted by stylised Corinthian capitals, sphinxes or fish. Finally, Egyptian influence is best seen in funerary stelae, which have survived in large number throughout Egypt. They are either square or rectangular in shape and are sometimes curved at the top, or have a triangular pediment. Many have a tiny square cavity, which penetrated to the back of the stele. Such cavities were common in ancient Egyptian cemeteries, and incense was burned in them in the belief that the spirit of the dead would enjoy its perfume. In the early Christian era stelae came from pagan and Christian burial grounds, and were usually inscribed with the name of the deceased, details of his life or titles, and the day of his death, written in Greek or Coptic. The

68

carvings on them included Greek-Egyptian motifs: a figure, often robed like an aristocratic Greek reclining on a bed and holding a drinking vessel or grapes, for example, might be flanked by the jackal-god Anubis and the hawk-headed Horus.

The persistence of ancient Egyptian symbolism in early Christian art remains a controversial issue among biblical historians who do not recognise evidence of "pagan" inspiration in Christian art. It is accepted that the ansate cross, the *ankh* or hieroglyphic sign for the word 'life', was intentionally adopted by the early Christians. In fact, many relief slabs show both the *ankh* and the Christian cross together, frequently flanked by the first and last letters of the Greek alphabet, the alpha and omega, in an early form of what was to become the monogram of Christ. Other examples of Egyptian symbolism in early Christian art are the Spirit or Holy Ghost in the early church shown descending in the form of a winged bird, like the soul of the deceased, the *ba*, in ancient Egypt; the archangel Michael weighing souls in the balance, which is akin to the ancient Egyptian god of wisdom, Thoth, weighing the heart of the deceased in the scales of justice; the portrayal of Christ triumphant over noxious beasts is evidently derived from that of Horus upon the crocodiles, as shown on the famous Metternich stele. And Saint George and the dragon also call to mind the god Horus depicted spearing Set, often portrayed as an evil serpent.

In addition to the classical, Egyptian and Greek-Egyptian heritages in Coptic art, there are also Persian, Byzantine and Syrian influences. Egyptian master weavers and artists were attracted to Persia in the third century with the rise of the Sassanian kingdom before the founding of Constantinople. When they returned, a new Persian repertory of themes like opposing horsemen or two facing peacocks drinking out of the same vessel, was introduced to Egypt. Borrowing from one culture to another is a natural process of cultural growth. In the fourth century, when Christianity made a triumphal entry into the Roman world the art forms of ascendant Byzantium spread to Egypt, and continued even after the Coptic Church broke away from the Eastern Roman Church because Egypt remained, politically, a part of the Roman Empire. The Copts, however, were disenchanted with Alexandria as the centre of culture (despite it being the city of Saint Mark's martyrdom) because it was associated with the Eastern Church. They began to turn increasingly towards the Holy Land, the birthplace of Jesus Christ; Syrian influence on Coptic art became apparent in the fifth century. And, as the more forceful, orientalised style penetrated Egypt, a certain rigidity came with it. Some motifs that made their way to Egypt from Syria were ultimately of Persian origin, including animals and birds in roundels, and griffins.

The integration of contrasting configurations—classical, Egyptian, Greek-Egyptian and Persian pagan motifs, as well as Byzantine and Syrian Christian influence—led to a trend in Coptic art that is difficult to define, because a unity of style is not possible to trace. Unfortunately, early collections of Christian art were made without recording details of the sites from which they came, making it virtually impossible to trace artistic development through time. There is no way to tell, for example, how long classical and Greek-Egyptian motifs continued after the adoption of Christianity as the state religion of the Roman Empire. All that can be said is that Coptic art is a distinctive art, and that it differed from that of Antioch, Constantinople and Rome.

In studying the objects in the Coptic Museum as well as the various monastic centres, it seems possible that sophisticated work was produced by highly talented craftsmen at the same time as work that is characterised by folk simplicity. This can be seen in ivory-work, tapestries, paintings and architectural decorations. It is tempting to link this dichotomy with the schism in religious beliefs between the Melkites, who enjoyed royal patronage, and the Monophysites, who did not. But there is another possible, more plausible, explanation.

Egypt had a long tradition of master craftsmen of different trades who, throughout ancient history, worked under the direction of a supervisor who was a highly professional man: sometimes a High Priest (as in the Old Kingdom) or an Overseer of All the Works of the King (New Kingdom). The supervisor could recognise inferior workmanship, correct drawings and generally maintain the required standard, whatever that happened to be during different periods. If there were changes in theme or style, this could only be brought about by the master craftsman who was empowered to execute the change. Naturally such a man had experience in handling large groups of men. Throughout the period of Roman rule of Egypt there was a tendency for such master craftsmen to move around the Roman Empire, gravitating towards the centres that could pay for their professional services. They worked in Alexandria and were summoned by the emperors to Rome and Constantinople. There they sculpted classically draped forms as competently as they had the stylised Egyptian, and they carved languid reclining figures with no less devotion. Scholars are not in agreement over which works of art can safely be regarded as Alexandrine – that is to say, executed by Egyptian craftsmen in Alexandria. Only a few can be safely attributed to Egypt through consideration of subject matter or style. They include a casket now in the museum in Wiesbaden that is sculpted with a sphinx and the allegory of Father Nile, a small box in the British Museum showing the squat, typically Coptic figure of Saint Menas in a niche, and three plaques from the side of Maximianus' throne at Ravenna Museum that have been attributed by art historians to Egyptian carvers. Also, when the Copts separated from the Eastern church, master craftsmen who had worked for Byzantine patrons continued to do so. They had mastered the technique of deeper drill carving and supervised the execution of works of great sophistication, *vide* the stucco wall decorations to be found in the Monastery of the Syrians at Wadi Natrun and the friezes from Bawit in the Coptic Museum.

Meanwhile, however, monasteries and churches that were built in Upper Egypt, especially in the fifth and sixth centuries, were adorned with carvings and paintings that show an expression of faith that was highly personal, executed by craftsmen who were not controlled by either the rulings of the church, or by a supervisor who maintained standards. There are stone and wood friezes, painted panels and ivory work that is crude and that depends for its appeal largely on qualities of design. This is especially apparent in the representations of the human figure, which are of strange pro-

71

portion, being somewhat squat with large heads. A convincing explanation for this has yet to be made. It has been suggested that Coptic artists were producing work in reaction to the realism of ancient Egyptian and Greek paganism and that this, too, is the reason why the early Christians did not encourage the production of statuary in the round. While the tendency seems, indeed, to have been a departure from Hellenistic Alexandrine tradition, towards an abstract two-dimensional style, this may not necessarily have been calculated. Rather, it may be an example of free artistic expression: naive, unsophisticated, yet forceful.

Efforts have been made to classify Coptic art into epochs but this is somewhat artificial. While every culture has phases of cultural production, this is visible only when seen from an historical vantage. E.R. Dodds comments: "The practice of chopping history into convenient lengths and calling them 'periods' or 'ages' has . . . drawbacks. Strictly speaking, there are no periods in history, only in historians; actual history is a smoothly flowing continuum, a day following a day." (*Pagan & Christian in an Age of Anxiety*, p.3).

This is true of art. Day by day, through the centuries of Ptolemaic rule, while Greek culture became inextricable from the ancient Egyptian, a national heritage yet remained. This apparent contradiction is best exemplified by referring to the literature of the Late Period, in which such syncretistic compilations as the Hermetic texts (see *Introduction*) developed alongside a more or less consistent pattern of thought and behaviour, as exemplified in the Instruction literature (chapter one). In art, the diverse influences resulted in an admixture of motifs. Yet, despite this, distinctive "Egyptian" traits set Coptic art apart from any other.

No other early Christian movement has such an abundance of paintings of persons who received honour in their own country. Egypt's martyrs, saints, patriarchs, hermits and ascetics, some of whom were honoured throughout the Christian world, received special distinction in Egypt. Their heroic deeds, sufferings or miracles were told in legend, their relics became the focus of worship and, in accordance with ancient traditions, places of healing. Sometimes, in ancient temples that were converted to chapels or churches,

72

a row of venerated hermits, monks and the founders of monasteries were depicted on the plastered walls that once covered rows of ancient Egyptian deities carved in relief.

The human figures, whether in paintings, carvings or tapestries, are in frontal position with serene faces and a depth of idealised expression. The outlined, almond-shaped eyes are strongly reminiscent of the painted wooden panels from Bawit and the Fayoum, dating to the first and second centuries, which were placed over the head of the deceased and bound into the mummy wrappings. These panels themselves resemble *cartonnage* sarcophagi of the late pharaonic period. In fact, the Fayoum portraits, with the full face and large obsessive eyes — a feature of Roman medallions and much early Christian art — are now regarded by art historians as the prototypes for the Byzantine icons.

Jesus Christ was usually shown enthroned, surrounded by triumphant saints or angels, or blessing a figure beside Him. He was always depicted as King, never the suffering servant. Egypt was a land where leadership was idealised and kingship, both on earth and in the afterlife, was something the people understood. A triumphant Jesus — reborn, benevolent and righteous — is one of the most significant and continuous characteristics of Coptic art. Another is that Egyptians did not delight in painting scenes of torture, death or sinners in hell; in the few exceptions where a holy man is painted undergoing torture, it is implied rather than graphically depicted. This is in tune with ancient Egyptian artistic tradition which, in the words of Cyril Aldred, tended to "magnify only the heroic and beneficent qualities of divinities and kings, and not the horrific power of tyrants and demons." (*Egyptian Art in the Days of the Pharaohs*, Thames and Hudson, 1980, p. 12)

The study of Coptic art and archicture was for too long a sadly neglected field. One of the reasons for this is that early archaeologists showed no interest in Christian antiquities. They regarded Coptic art as decadent, dull and non-classical. It is astonishing to us today to note that Champollion, the French scholar who deciphered hieroglyphics from the famous Rosetta Stone, carried out excavations at Medinet Habu on the Theban necropolis, discovered

73

a fine fifth century church there and did not even mention it in his official report. In places where ancient Egyptian temples had been converted into churches and the walls plastered and painted with Christian themes, these were removed as just so much debris obscuring the ancient Egyptian reliefs below. No effort was made to photograph the wall-paintings before removal, or record any architectural features. Vital evidence was consequently lost from numerous temples including Deir el Bahri, Medinet Habu and Karnak temples at Luxor, and those of Dendera and Edfu.

The first person to realise the value of Coptic art and make an effort to preserve it was the French scholar Gaston Maspero. In 1881, in his capacity as director of the Egyptian Antiquities Service (now Antiquities Organisation) he set aside one of the halls of the Museum of Antiquities, then in the suburb of Boulac, for the first collection of Coptic art. He encouraged Egyptologists to undertake serious excavation, resulting in the preservation of the remains of the Monastery of Saint Apollo in Bawit, about fifteen kilometres south-west of Assiut in Middle Egypt, and the Monastery of Saint Jeremias on the Sakkara plateau. Several scholars published descriptions of Coptic churches, carvings and crafts, but with no surviving churches of the early centuries, and with professional emphasis on dated material, this automatically imposed certain restrictions.

In 1910 the Coptic Museum (chapter five) was founded and in 1937 a new wing was added. The exhibits, which represent the richest collection of Coptic art in the world, have been separated according to media: stonework, woodwork, metalwork, ivory carvings, tapestries, pottery, glassware and manuscripts. It is extremely difficult to visualise them in context when one visits the museum. For example, patriarchal chairs in woodwork in the old wing are separated from patriarchal crowns and ecclesiastical vestments that are in the new. Wooden doors of ancient churches and monasteries are separated from their metal bolts and keys. Similar themes in different mediums, like the portrayal of the Virgin and Child, or the use of vine as a decorative motif in stone carvings, wooden panels and tapestries, cannot be compared. And wide variations in style that developed in different localities cannot be observed. Compounding the problem is the fact that the objects span fifteen hundred years, from the fourth to the nineteenth centuries!

Nor do the monastic centres of Egypt facilitate an understanding of artistic development because of the continuous stages of construction and renovation of the churches. For example, the famous monasteries of Wadi Natrun were affected by the factional disputes during the fourth century and, in the fifth century, the Melkite monks from Alexandria managed to oust the Copts. The Melkites remained in occupation until the Arab conquest when the Copts took over the area again. Each transfer heralded art and architectural activities. Then, in the eighth century one of the monasteries was purchased and restored by a Syrian. There were serious Bedouin raids from the eighth to the eleventh centuries and a great deal of damage was done to the ancient buildings. They were restored in Fatimid times, eleventh and twelfth centuries, and the Fatimids themselves used local craftsmen, who were mostly Copts, for enlarging and embellishing the city of Cairo; when Copts executed designs and motifs that were acceptable to their Arab patrons, they did this as competently as they had, in classical times, produced classical themes for Greek patrons. In each case they adopted some of the motifs or designs for their own use. Therefore, when one visits the monasteries of Wadi Natrun, it must be borne in mind that some wall-paintings were produced under the Monophysite monks, others under the Melkites. Also, Alexandrine, Byzantine and Syrian-inspired art were produced there, as well as non-figurative metalwork, wooden sanctuary screens, cabinets and furniture, inspired by Islam.

There are two art forms in which continuity of craftsmanship can be traced, namely the techniques of weaving and illustration. That is to say, Coptic textiles and manuscripts. While the motifs in the former, and the calligraphy in the latter, changed from age to age, the artistic execution of the work, as well as the techniques and the materials used, was of longstanding tradition.

Weaving in the early Christian era was, as in earlier times, mainly on linen although there is also some evidence of silkweaving. The techniques — the so-called tapestry-weave and loom weaving — were inherited from the ancient Egyptians. The width of the loom used in Coptic tapestries (and later for the weaving of Islamic fabrics) is the same as that in the time of the pharaohs, and the special "Egyptian knot" was used as well. In the fourth century wool was introduced and a variant was loopweaving, in which the waft was not pulled tight. Silk became popular in the sixth century and by the eighth century full clerical tunics were woven in linen and silk. The weaving of some are so fine as to appear more like embroidery.

Coptic textiles, which developed into one of the finest of all Coptic arts, included wall hangings, blankets and curtains in addition to garment trimmings. The motifs show great diversity and include classical and Greek-Egyptian themes: lively cupids, dancing girls riding marine monsters, or birds and animals woven into foliage. Fish and grapes were popular Christian motifs as well as biblical scenes such as the Virgin on a donkey holding the Child Jesus in front of her. After Constantinople became the capital of the empire, the weavers' repertoire was increased and enriched with Byzantine and Persian themes. All the textiles show a great sense of liveliness in the stylised figures, and there was an eager market throughout the Roman world in late antiquity, especially for trimmings for clerical robes; the most commonly woven were tunics of undyed linen onto which decorative woven bands were worked. After the Arab conquest, Copts wove textiles for Muslim patrons and the Arab *kufic* script was introduced into their own designs, especially after Arabic replaced the Coptic language.

Coptic manuscripts fall into five main groups: in Greek, Greek and Coptic, in Coptic, Coptic and Arabic and, finally, in Arabic. The art of illustrating texts dates to pharaonic times when prayers and liturgies were written on papyrus paper with reed pens and deposited in the tomb of the deceased. The mortuary texts were traced in black outline with catchwords written in red. They were illustrated with figures of Egyptian deities and protective symbols. These vignettes were frequently painted in bright colours with border designs at the top and bottom.

In the Christian era, religious writings were also written on papyrus paper and parchment. The texts were written in black, with red

76

used for the titles and the beginnings of the chapters. Many were decorated with designs in bright colours including figures of martyrs, saints, apostles and angels as well as birds, animals, foliage and geometrical designs. A medieval writer, Omar Tussun, wrote about a group of copyists at the Monastery of Saint Makar in Wadi Natrun, who were capable of drawing Coptic letters in the form of birds and figures. This is still an art form in Egypt, and Arabic caligraphers still use the reed pen. Copts started to translate their religious literature into Arabic in the twelfth century and decorated the opening page with lavish pictures and with border designs.

It is fitting to conclude this chapter with Coptic paintings, which is true art as against what we today call the crafts. The wall paintings reveal an unsophisticated, almost crude style and a refined, highly developed one. The former may have emerged in the early years of Christianity when ancient temples were converted into churches. Pharaonic reliefs were covered with layers of plaster and Christian themes were painted on the stucco base. These wall-paintings survive *in situ* in some places in Egypt including Bagawat in Kharga Oasis, Saint Simeon's Monastery at Aswan, in the Temple of Luxor, the White Monastery at Sohag, the Monastery of Saint Makar in Wadi Natrun, and the sanctuary of the Ethiopian saint Takla Hamanout in the Church of Al Moallaka in Old Cairo. Early wall-paintings that have been transferred to the Coptic Museum include niches from the monasteries of Bawit and Sakkara. The Copts loved bright, clear colour and were extremely talented in mixing different dyes and powdered rock, often using the white of an egg to combine them.

Icons, or images of sacred personalities painted on wooden panels, that are themselves regarded as sacred, were a later development. When it was realised that the war on paganism launched by the emperor Theodosius had not stopped pious people from sanctifying holy relics, the church authorised the painting of religious themes that would aid the faithful in an understanding of Christianity, especially scenes depicting the Nativity, the Virgin and Child, the apostles and the lives of the saints. According to al-Makrizi, the Arab historian, the patriarch Cyril I hung icons in all

77

the churches of Alexandria in the year 420 and then decreed that they should be hung in the other churches of Egypt as well.

In the earliest development of icon painting the artists worked directly on the wooden panel but later they began to cover the surface with a soft layer of gypsum onto which lines could be chiselled to control the flow of liquid gold. There is indication that more than one artist was involved in the production of a single work but the face was painted by the master. Such division of labour resulted in greater production, but it also brought an end to any personal expression of piety such as had characterised the wall-paintings. When Egypt turned increasingly towards Syria and Palestine after the schism in the fifth century, her saints and martyrs began to take on the stiff, majestic look of Syrian art. There began to be an expression of spirituality rather than naivety on the faces of the subjects, more elegance in the drawing of the figures, more use of gold backgrounds and richly adorned clerical garments.

Painters were not, at first, constrained by a rigid code. They were free to experiment with their themes. Consequently, there is a variety of interpretations in the treatment of a single subject that is quite striking. By the fifth and sixth centuries the angel Gabriel, for example, was sometimes painted with a sword, another time with a cross and, on occasion, with a trumpet; he either wore a flowing robe or was clad in richly embroidered vestments. Such variations are especially notable in scenes of the Annunciation and the Nativity, which are seldom rendered twice with the same details.

Paintings produced in Egypt under Byzantine rule did not resemble the opulent frescoes and mosaics of the eastern Roman Empire, which was state-sponsored art between 550 and the conquest of the Turks in the fifteenth century. Saint Catherine's Monastery in Sinai, however, a stronghold of the Melkite faction, was rebuilt in the Golden Age of Justinian and adorned with some of the finest Byzantine icons to be found in the world. Some were painted on site, and others were imported from the provinces of the empire and from Constantinople itself.

After the Arab conquest of Egypt in the seventh century paintings became successively less "Coptic" in character. This became even more apparent in the thirteenth century when the art of copying panels and miniatures started and Anba Gabriel produced exquisite and brilliantly adorned work. He set a standard for copyists. Little original work was produced. By the seventeenth and eighteenth centuries painters like John el-Nassikh, Baghdady (literally "of Baghdad") Abu el-Saad, and John the Armenian—who are among the greatest painters of icons in Egypt—turned to Syrian and Byzantine models for inspiration. Finally, Anastasy, a Greek artist, was commissioned by the Copts to paint many of the icons that today hang in the churches of Old Cairo.

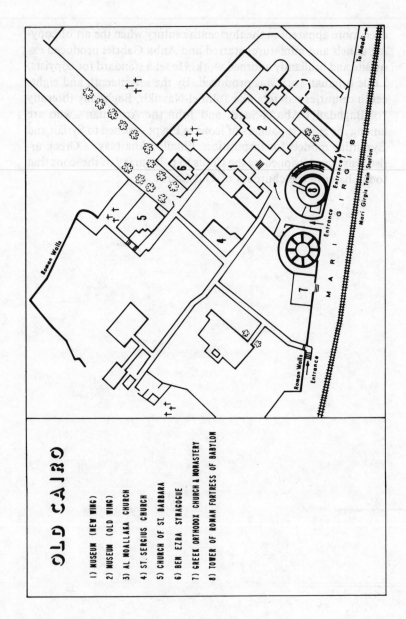

OLD CAIRO

1) MUSEUM (NEW WING)
2) MUSEUM (OLD WING)
3) AL MOALLAKA CHURCH
4) ST. SERGIUS CHURCH
5) CHURCH OF ST BARBARA
6) BEN EZRA SYNAGOGUE
7) GREEK ORTHODOX CHURCH & MONASTERY
8) TOWER OF ROMAN FORTRESS OF BABYLON

4

OLD CAIRO

Old Cairo, *Masr el Qadima*, lies within the old Roman fortress of Babylon. It was not only a walled but a heavily fortified city with narrow streets and cobbled alleys. How the name of the famous Babylon of the Euphrates came to be echoed in Egypt is not known. The Coptic historian John of Nikou, who lived at the time of the Arab invasion, claimed that it was originally built during the Persian occupation of Egypt, 525–332 BC, and that it was at that time called the Fortress of Babylon. However, a much earlier visitor to the land of the Nile, the classical writer Diodorus Siculus, asserted that the name was brought by prisoners of war from great Babylon; the Twelfth Dynasty pharaoh Senusert, some 2000 years BC, brought them to build public works. These Babylonians, he claimed, revolted against the Egyptians and built a fortification for protection, which had long fallen to ruin when the Persians came and repaired it.

When the Roman geographer Strabo came to Egypt early in the Christian era, he found that Old Cairo was, indeed, a fortress town and was occupied by three Roman garrisons. The emperor Trajan (98–117), it was said, cleared a canal that was running through the city and included some urban areas, into the enlarged fortress. Moreover, he cleared a canal connecting the Nile with the Red Sea; it had originally been dug by the pharaohs of the Twenty-sixth Dynasty, about 600 BC, and was revealed to him by the Egyptians. By this time the area was known as the "Castle of Babylon." Under the Christian emperor Arcadius (395–408), the Copts began to build numerous churches in Old Cairo. Forty-two are believed to have once stood in an area of about sixty acres, which extended northwards as far as today's Ezbekieh Gardens, near Opera Square.

At the time of the Arab conquest in 641, Babylon was such a

81

sizable community that part of the fortress, including the huge towers and bastions, was connected by walls to the newly founded Arab capital of Fustat. These towers as well as the bastions were at first used as dwellings for the garrison. Later Amr ibn al-As, leader of the Arabs at the time of the conquest, returned to the Copts land that the Imperial government had taken from them. Forthwith the whole of Old Cairo became inhabited exclusively by Copts and the Arabs recruited local labour from their ranks.

Coptic churches were rebuilt and restored time and again over the centuries, often re-using wood and stone-work. For this reason some parts of a church may be of earlier date than the structure itself. Although they differ in size and architectural features they bear the unmistakable stamp of a Coptic church. The exteriors are characterised by great simplicity and are often indistinguishable from neighbouring, unadorned, brick dwellings flanking a cobbled street. The axis of the building runs east to west with the entrance to the west and the high altar placed in the east nearest the rising run.

The interior of the early churches has a simple ground plan in four main divisions: the forecourt or narthex, the main body of the church with the nave higher than the side aisles, a porch or transept and the inner chambers. The nave, which has an arched timber roof, is separated from the side aisles by columns with supporting arches, enabling a second row of columns to be superimposed on them and providing light from the clerestory. The columns, frequently taken from earlier Greek or Roman buildings, had their shafts painted with figures of saints. The side aisles are also arched with timber but are at a lower level.

There was originally a low parapet with curtains separating the main body of the church from the sanctuary, which is usually erected on rising ground and ascended by a few steps. Later the parapet became a rail or screen beyond which only those in holy orders may pass. The sanctuary screen is made of wood, decorated with geometrical segments of ebony and ivory, often of intricate workmanship. Behind the screen are three domed apses or *haikals*. The central apse holds the altar of the saint to whom the church

82

is dedicated and the two wide apses are used either on the saint's feast day or whenever there is more than one celebration of the divine liturgy on such occasions as Easter, Christmas and Palm Sunday. Coptic altars are free-standing and in the middle of the chapel. Above the altar is a wooden canopy resting on pillars. The side chambers are sometimes raised above the level of the choir but the altar, with few exceptions, stands level with the floor. Behind the central altar there is a tribunal with a throne for a bishop and seats for the officiating clergy. A niche in the wall usually holds a sanctuary lamp, known as the perpetual lamp.

In the early years of Christianity, it was customary to bury the bodies of saints or martyrs beneath the altar, either in a vault or in a crypt beneath the floor of the sanctuary. All Coptic churches still possess relics, which are enclosed in a casket beneath a silk brocade or kept beneath glass beside a picture of the patron saint. They are never on display. Some of the desert churches that date to the Middle Ages have reliquaries containing entire bodies but it was more usual for the relics to be clothing of the saint, pieces of bone, hair or even teeth. When the relics are in portable caskets, they can be removed and carried in procession for the healing of the sick or for important religious celebrations.

One of the earliest surviving churches, the Church of Abu Sarga, was planned along the earliest known arrangement for church rituals. A candidate for baptism was first received in a small ante chamber and then descended three steps into the baptistry, where he was immersed in water. When the rite was completed he received the eucharist and only then was allowed to enter the church. Purification *before* entering a holy place (a temple was called *hut neter*, "house (of) god") was of ancient origin. Only later was the baptistry moved to the side of the narthex of a church (but still before the nave and aisles) and later still it was constructed at the end of the northern aisle near the altar. Today, scarcely a church in Egypt has its baptistry outside the main part of the church. In the narthex of some ancient churches there is an oblong tank sunk in the floor, now covered with floorboards. This was originally used for libation or blessing of water, for which service a portable basin is now

83

used. Similarly, a shallow rectangular basin, also sunk in the floor, was used for the foot-washing service on Maundy Thursday and on the feast of the Saints Peter and Paul. The baptistry is now generally situated at the upper end of the northern aisle of the church. The front is a basin deep enough to allow the priest to immerse the child totally in water while pronouncing the baptismal formulary.

The pulpits of a Coptic church have a distinctive straight-sided balcony attached to a circular platform. The polygonal pulpits found at Wadi Natrun, for example, are rare in Coptic churches and are inevitably of modern date. The lectern usually stands before the door to the sanctuary. It is made of wood, sometimes inlaid with geometrical designs in ivory. The use of the ostrich egg in Coptic churches, hung in front of the sanctuary screen and regarded as an emblem of the resurrection, is of uncertain origin. Copts explain that they symbolise the vigilance with which an ostrich ceaselessly protects its egg, and is consequently meant to remind the congregation that their thoughts should be on spiritual matters. Another explanation may be rooted in tradition: the myth of the origin of life from an egg is recurrent in ancient Egyptian mythology, especially the primordial egg from which life began. Ostrich eggs, and pottery eggs, are still used as decorative elements in churches, and in mosques.

Description. Old Cairo lies south of Cairo, opposite the southern tip of Roda Island. The railway station of Mari Girgis, which gives onto a street of the same name, is almost opposite the two towers of the old Roman fortress, between which is the gateway leading to the Coptic Museum (chapter five). Built on top of the northern tower is the Greek Orthodox Church of Mari Girgis. The southern tower has recently been cleared and the original walls of the fortress can be seen. They are of dressed stone with alternating courses of bricks. Some of the stones in the tower, and also the buildings of Old Cairo, bear hieroglyphic inscriptions attesting to the re-use of stone from ancient Egyptian temples. The famous Coptic Church of Al Moallaka lies immediately to the south of the tower and is approached from the main road.

The Church of Al Moallaka. This church is known as the "Hanging" or "Suspended" Church because it rests on the two southwestern bastions of the old Roman fortress of Babylon. Its nave extends over the rampart that led into the ancient fortress. Some parts of the original church still survive, notably the section that lies to the right of the sanctuary, on top of the southern bastion of the fortress.

The Church of Al Moallaka was the seat of the Bishop of Babylon (i.e., Cairo) in the seventh century. In the ninth century it was destroyed but when the church was restored in the eleventh century, it was made the seat of the Coptic Patriarchate. At this time it became the centre to which theologians, lawyers and astronomers came for study. The church underwent periodic renovation from medieval right through to modern times. Some of the wood and stone-work were re-used so that they date to an earlier period than the structure in which they are housed. Also, some parts of this church, and others in Old Cairo, have been taken to the Coptic Museum: for example, a sycamore panel found over the doorway of Al Moallaka Church, and the pinewood altar-dome from the Church of Abu Sarga.

The entrance gateway to Al Moallaka Church leads to a stairway, which gives onto a passage and a covered courtyard. The outer porch is decorated with glazed tiles in Islamic geometrical designs.

The main part of the church has a wide central nave and narrow side aisles, separated by eight columns on each side. The vaulted timber roof has recently been restored. The columns have Corinthian capitals, indicating their having been usurped from earlier buildings. With one exception, in black basalt, the columns are of white marble. They were once painted with figures of saints but only a single column still bears the traces of a figure and it is badly faded. There are three other columns in the centre of the nave, to the right of which is the pulpit. It is made of marble and is supported by fif-

85

teen slender columns that feature different twisted or fluted decorations. The pulpit in Al Moallaka Church, with its straight-sided balcony, is thought to be among the earliest surviving. It is assigned to the eleventh century but some of the material of which it is made may be earlier. It is of marble and rests on fifteen delicate columns arranged in seven pairs with a leader, symbolising the seven sacraments of the church. Each pair is identical, but no two pairs are alike.

The inlaid woodwork of this church is among the finest to be found. Cedarwood and ivory were used for the sanctuary screen. The ivory is carved into segments of exquisite design and set in the woodwork to form the Coptic cross; like the Spanish cross the Coptic has arms of even length and three end points symbolising the Blessed Trinity. At the top of the sanctuary screen are a series of icons of saints representing Christ enthroned, at the centre, with the Virgin, the archangel Gabriel and Saint Peter to the right, and Saint John the Baptist, the archangel Michael and Saint Paul to the left.

Behind the sanctuary screen is the altar. High altars in Coptic churches are covered with a canopy resting on four columns. The side altars are sometimes similarly covered. The central altar of Al Moallaka is dedicated to the Blessed Virgin and the side altars to and Saint John the Baptist to the right, and Saint George to the left. The latter, a Roman legionary, defied Diocletian and suffered martyrdom in Asia. His body was said to have been brought to Egypt by the Coptic patriarch Gabriel II in the twelfth century.

A small church dedicated to Takla Hamanout, the Ethiopian saint, leads off of the main church of Al Moallaka, to the right, near the transept. The screen that separates it from the main church is worthy of note. It is regarded as one of the finest pieces of craftsmanship and one of the highest examples of Coptic woodwork of the tenth century. It is made of wood and mother of pearl and when illuminated from behind with a candle, which is available for use, the segments glow with a rose tint.

Two wall-paintings in the chapel of the much venerated Ethiopian saint are noteworthy even though badly faded. One shows the

86

twenty-four elders of the Apocalypse, with halos surrounding their heads, standing in a row and the other is of the Virgin and Child situated in the extreme right-hand corner. They are believed to date to the twelfth or thirteenth century.

A small, newly restored stairway inside this chapel leads to another chapel on a higher level. It is thought to be the earliest part of the Church of Al Moallaka and it has been suggested that it may date to as early as the third century when the fortress walls were built. It is a small square chamber with four wooden columns. It is dedicated, by tradition, to Saint Mark.

The Church of Saint Sergius (Abu Sarga). The Church of Saint Sergius is one of the oldest surviving churches. It is situated to the north of the museum, down a narrow cobbled lane, and it lies some ten metres below the street level. The church is dedicated to two Roman Officers, Sergius and Bacchus, who were martyred in Syria in the reign of Maximian. The earliest part of the building dated to the fifth century and was built over the cave where, according to tradition, the Holy Family hid during their flight into Egypt. The structure was burnt down and restored in the eighth century. The whole of the church was again restored and partially rebuilt during the Fatimid era, the tenth to eleventh centuries. Despite restoration and reconstruction the Church of Saint Sergius is, nevertheless, regarded as a model of the early churches in which Copts worshipped.

The entrance is approached down a flight of stairs. It leads to the side of the narthex where there is a large basin, boarded over, formerly used for blessings during the feast of the Epiphany. At the end of the narthex is the baptistry. The nave of the church, which has an arched timber roof, is separated from the side aisles by marble pillars with supporting arches enabling a second row of columns to be superimposed on them. The figures that once blazoned the columns are only dimly discernible today. On the right-hand wall are fifteen icons of religious subjects including Christ's birth, miracles, baptism and ressurrection; they date to medieval times. There is an interesting eighth-century carving of the Last Supper.

87

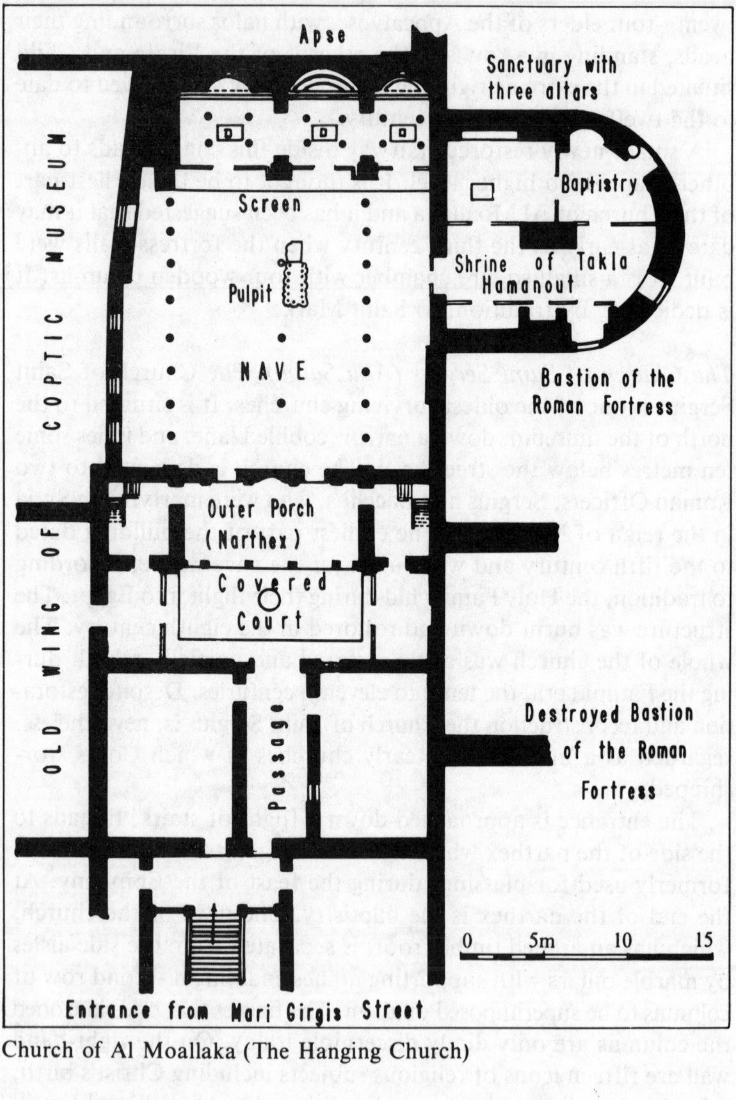
Apse
Sanctuary with three altars
Baptistry
Screen
Shrine of Takla Hamanout
Pulpit
NAVE
Bastion of the Roman Fortress
OLD WING OF COPTIC MUSEUM
Outer Porch (Narthex)
Covered Court
Destroyed Bastion of the Roman Fortress
Passage
0 5m 10 15
Entrance from Mari Girgis Street
Church of Al Moallaka (The Hanging Church)

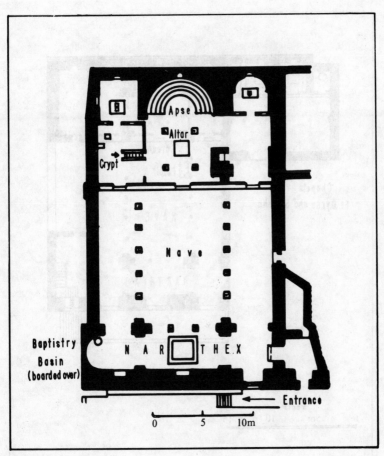

Church of St. Sergius

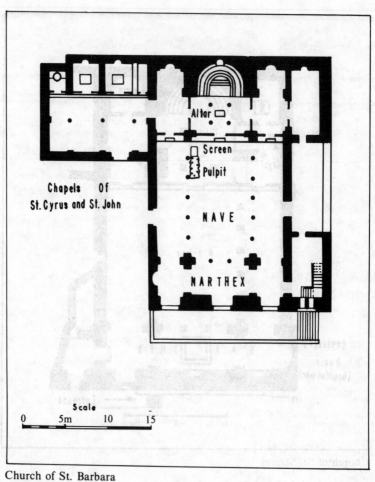

Church of St. Barbara

Jesus sits with his disciples at a table, which is of similar shape to an ancient Egyptian offering table. Indeed, a Coptic altar closely resembles an offering table. It has a raised moulding and a break in the border to drain off water.

The marble pulpit in the nave, which rests on ten columns, is a modern copy of the pulpit in the Church of Saint Barbara. Fragments of the original rosewood pulpit, inlaid with ebony and ivory, are now preserved in the Coptic Museum. The sanctuary screen is decorated with several panels, which may originally have come from the leaves of a door. The upper part contains small panels of ebony set with large crosses of solid ivory, exquisitely chiselled with scroll-work. Lower down the ivory is set in arabesque shapes. The icons are of the twelve apostles with the Virgin at the centre.

Brass oil lamps that hang from the ceiling and two steps lead up to the sanctuary and the side chapels. The original canopied altar is one of the treasures of the old wing of the Coptic Museum. The central apse wall is encrusted with marble and decorated in mosaics. Parts of the original paintings can still be seen in the dome. The side chapels contain numerous icons including one of the Flight into Egypt where Mary, shown on a mule, is wearing a crown and holding Jesus, followed by Joseph and Mary Magdalene.

The crypt, where the Holy Family are believed to have hidden during the flight into Egypt, lies to the left of the sanctuary. It is now inaccessible due to the level of the sub-soil water. The original cave was situated beneath the centre of the choir. It was built into a three-aisled chapel, with an altar in the wall in the form of a tomb-recess.

A commemorative mass is celebrated in the Church of Saint Sergius on June 1, which the Copts believe to be the day of the Flight.

Church of Saint Barbara. This church was originally dedicated to Saint Cyrus and Saint John (Abu Kir and Yuhanna in Arabic) and may date to as early as the fourth century. Abu Kir came from the city of Damanhour in the Delta and, according to legend, he and his brother agreed with two priests, one of whom was called Yuhan-

91

na, to go to the governor of the province and confess to having embraced Christianity. The governor commanded that they be shot with arrows, burned in a furnace, bound to the tails of horses and dragged to a neighbouring city. All was done but the saintly men suffered no harm. At last it was commanded that they be beheaded by sword outside the city of Damanhour. After the martyrdom some holy men came and built a church over the body of Abu Kir. The bodies of the other three saints were buried in Damanhour. Later, in the time of Cyrillus of Alexandria, the bodies of Abu Kir and Yuhanna were exhumed and transported to Alexandria to the Church of Saint Mark. Near this church there was an underground labyrinth where pagan worshippers honoured idols. When they saw the bodies of the saints and heard of the miracles, they converted to Christianity.

The church was re-built by a wealthy scribe in 684, destroyed by the great fire of Fustat in 750 and subsequently restored in the eleventh century. Later, when the relics of Saint Barbara were transported there, a new sanctuary was added to house her relics. Saint Barbara was a young woman of Nicomedia in Asia Minor who was killed by her father when she tried to convert him to Christianity.

The main part of this church, dedicated to Saint Barbara, is one the largest and finest in Egypt. It has the usual division of narthex, nave with side aisles and three apses or sanctuaries. The original sanctuary screen is in the Coptic Museum. The one in the church dates to the thirteenth century and is of wood inlaid with carved ivory. The icons are of the Virgin Mary, Jesus and saints. Behind the main altar is a domed apse that has seven steps decorated in bands of black, red and white marble.

The church dedicated to the two martyrs Cyrus and John form the extension to the left of the sanctuary. It is square and comprises a nave, transept, two sanctuaries and a baptistry, which has a polygonal font set into the masonry. The relics of the two saints are kept in this church. It is interesting to note, therefore, that one of the icons shows Cyrus and John together with their relic case.

The Synagogue of Ben Ezra. This synagogue was formerly the Church of Saint Michael, which dated from the eighth century. The Jewish community of Old Cairo, however, relate a tradition that before being converted into a church it had been a synagogue since the time of Moses. It was reputedly destroyed by the Romans and given to the Copts by the Arabs. The church was destroyed once again in the twelfth century and subsequently restored to the Jews. At this time the Rabbi of Jerusalem, Abraham Ben Ezra, constructed the synagogue which still bears his name. Many medieval travellers visited the synagogue and recorded that they saw there the *Torah* of Ezra the scribe.

This is the oldest surviving synagogue in Egypt. It is situated in a small garden and is in a fine state of preservation. From the outside it looks little different from the early churches of Old Cairo. Also, apart from some distinctive interior features, it has the same simplicity as a Coptic church. Most of the decorative work, especially in wood and mother of pearl, are of twelfth century date.

The Star of David adorns the central marble pulpit, known as the *bima*, which is double-sided. The *bima* was used for the reading of the scriptures, which were later rolled up and put away in cupboards in a wooden screen. Above the cupboard for the scriptures are the Ten Commandments. The seven-branched candlestick, the *menorah*, can be seen.

At the end of the nineteenth century when excavations were being conducted at the site numerous manuscripts were found, including what has become known as the Geniza Document, so called because it was found in the lumber-room (*genizah* in Arabic). It is a great part of the Hebrew Book of Ecclesiasticus and is regarded as one of the most remarkable literary discoveries in modern times as well as the most valuable archives of the Middle Ages. Complete renovation of the synagogue was started in 1983.

Convent of Saint George. This convent, which was described in glowing terms by al-Makrizi in the fifteenth century is today inhabited by about thirty nuns. A small door from the narrow, cobbled streets of Old Cairo leads into the peaceful courtyard. A stairway leads down to the most ancient part of the convent where there is a remarkable hall dating to the tenth century. It has a high ceiling and doors around the hall that give onto fourteen small cells. The shrine containing the icon of Saint George is approached through a wooden doorway, the leaves of which are of tremendous height. The custodians of the shrine are proud to display a chain, of uncertain origin, that they claim was used to tie up martyrs.

Convent of Saint Mercurius (Deir abu al-Saifain). This convent is outside the walls of Old Cairo. It is situated to the north of the street leading to the Mosque of Amr. About fifty nuns live in the walled enclosure that contains three churches: The Church of Saint Damiana, which has a mosaic of the saint and the forty-five virgins who were massacred in the reign of Diocletian, the Church of the Holy Virgin (*El Adra*) and the Church of Saint Mecurius after whom the whole convent is named.

Mercurius was, according to one tradition, a Roman legionary who defied the emperor Decius. According to another, he was given a sword by an angel to use against the barbarians. Later he suffered martyrdom and, in the time of Julian the Apostate, he appeared to the emperor in a vision. Julian was battling against the Persians and Mecurius slew him with a lance. *Abu al-Saifain* means "he of two swords" and the saint was so called because of his many battles. He is generally depicted brandishing two swords. He was buried in Palestine and his remains were transferred in the fifteenth century to Old Cairo.

The Church of Saint Mercurius was first mentioned in the time of the patriarch Abraham (975–978) as having been demolished and turned into a storage area for sugar-cane. It was referred to again in the twelfth century, when it was rebuilt after having been attacked and burned by fanatical mobs. The church is remarkable for its icons, its fine sanctuary screen and a marble pulpit, which is decorated with mosaics and rests on fifteen columns. The ancient door of the cloister, made of sycamore wood strengthened by bands of iron, is in the old wing of the Coptic Museum.

5

THE COPTIC MUSEUM

The Coptic Museum in Old Cairo, which possesses the richest collection of Coptic art in the world, lies within the old Roman fortress of Babylon. It was founded in 1910 by Morcos Simaika, a wealthy Copt who felt that a special building should be devoted to Coptic antiquities. He raised funds by public subscription and used his personal influence to acquire important artifacts from old Coptic houses. The museum was built on land belonging to the Coptic patriarchate. In 1931 the Egyptian Government gave it official recognition and sympathetic support. The new wing was built in 1947 and two years later the collection hitherto in the Cairo Museum was transferred there. In 1983–84 the Coptic Museum was completely renovated as part of the restoration programme set in motion by the Organisation of Antiquities under Dr. Ahmed Kadry.

The monuments in the Coptic Museum are a bridge between the Cairo Museum of (Pharaonic) Antiquities, the Graeco-Roman Museum in Alexandria (which has some Coptic exhibits) and the Islamic Museum in Cairo. The objects have been grouped according to media: stonework, metalwork, tapestries and manuscripts in the new wing, and woodwork, pottery, glassware in the old.

The museum is approached from an elegantly laid-out garden with gazebos and benches. There are some fine pieces of decorative stonework in the garden, including an open-work limestone window decoration with floral designs in relief surrounding an Asian elephant at the centre. This and most of the other monuments in the garden are of uncertain date and provenance.

New Wing. A flight of stairs leads down to the entrance to the museum. The ground floor of the new wing is devoted to stone objects and wall-paintings from monasteries in Middle and Upper Egypt.

Chamber A contains niches and carvings that come from Ihnasia, near Beni Suef in Middle Egypt. They were found in the rubble of a churchyard and were overlooked for many years. They date to the fourth and fifth centuries of the Christian era but the subject matter is, nevertheless, typical of a pagan Greek community. Each piece is carved with mythological characters and motifs: the nude figures of Aphrodite in a shell, Leda and the swan, Europa and the bull, Dionysos with bunches of grapes and the goat-hoofed Pan seducing a dancer holding a systrum, to mention a few. Although the subject matter is wholly classical, with no Christian symbolism whatsoever, they are typically Coptic in spirit. That is to say, the style is distinct from that of similar reliefs to be found in Alexandria, Rome and Constantinople. The carvings from Ehnasia are more crudely done and have certain distinctive characteristics that point to their execution by Coptic artists, like the front-view faces with large, expressive eyes.

Chamber B contains more niches and stelae of the same period, but from a Christian burial ground. The use of classical and Egyptian symbolism is clear. For example, a pair of dolphins remain but in place of a sea-nymph at the centre there is a cross. A man with a child in his arms has a cross in the form of an ancient Egyptian *ankh*, or Key of Life, above his head. On the left-hand wall of the chamber there is evidence of the development of the cross in Egypt; some of the early examples are identical with the *ankh*, while others are variants of it, and one shows the *ankh* with a cross inside the loop at the top. Egyptian influence is also clear on the limestone fragment at the centre of the wall that shows the deceased lying on a bier with two figures, one at the head and one at the feet, much as the goddesses Isis and Nepthys are depicted at each end of ancient sarcophagi. The column at the centre of the chamber combines Byzantine and Egyptian decorative motifs: the squarish capital is carved in basket-weave with a cross on each side and is clearly Byzantine in character but at each corner are carvings of the hawk-headed Horus of ancient Egypt.

96

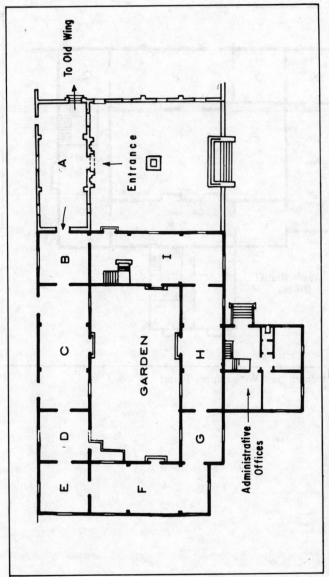

Coptic Museum New Wing (Ground Floor)

97

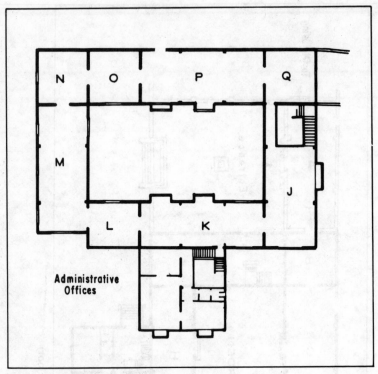

Coptic Museum New Wing (Upper Floor)

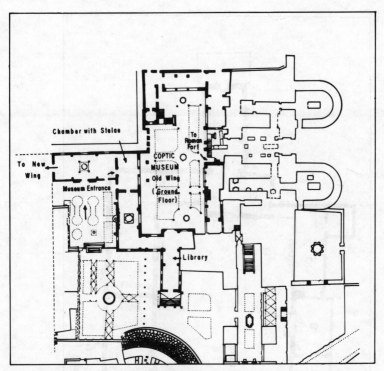

Coptic Museum Old Wing (Ground Floor)

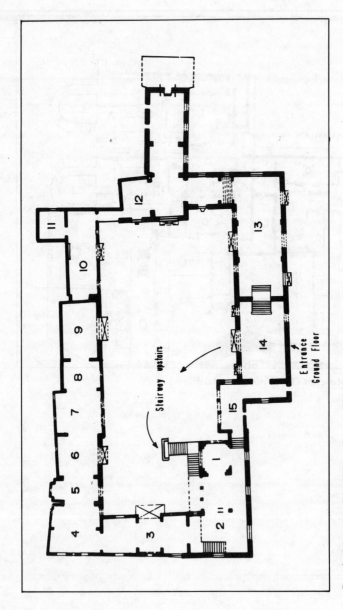

Coptic Museum Old Wing (Upper Floor)

Most of the monuments in chamber C come from Bawit, south-west of Dairut, which was a large monastery founded in the fifth century and inhabited until the eleventh. The stone objects include rather crudely carved panels, such as a bust of Christ held by flying angels that probably dates to the fifth or sixth centuries. On the other hand, the friezes which show great skill in the execution of geometric designs and foliage, may date to a later phase of construction. These friezes represent non-figural work of real quality.

At the centre of the right-hand wall is the main apse of the church painted in clear, bright colours. The upper part shows Christ enthroned, supported by the four creatures of the Apocalypse. The two faces shown in circles on each side of Christ are thought to indicate the sun (light) and the moon (dark). In the lower register the Virgin is painted with the Child on her lap. They are flanked by the apostles and two local saints. All the figures face forward and the names of the apostles and saints are written in Coptic above their heads.

Chamber D contains miscellaneous objects with classical motifs. The top of a limestone niche, for example, is carved in high relief and shows two plump naked infants with curly hair, carrying a cross that is encircled with a garland. Another shows an eagle carved with widespread wings and the bust of a saint above its head; the eagle became regarded as a symbol of the resurrection in early Christianity due to its periodically renewing its plumage (" . . . thy youth is renewed like an eagle's." Psalm 103:5).

Chamber E has a limestone freize with Coptic inscriptions arranged in two long rows of high relief. They are deeply carved by the hand of a master craftsman and exquisitely finished. In this chamber there are also some elaborately worked capitals of columns, one of which is carved with a double row of acanthus leaves that still bear traces of green colour. All the columns were once painted. The acanthus plant was an extremely popular architectural motif. One capital is decorated with leaves and branches that appear to be swayed by the wind.

All the monuments in chamber F come from the Monastery of Saint Jeremias at Sakkara, which was built in the fifth century. The

101

site was first excavated in 1907 and re-excavated and studied by Dr. P. Grossman of the German Archaeological Institute in 1980–81. The columns are arranged in pairs the full length of the hall and their deeply-carved capitals decorated with acanthus leaves, palm-fronds, the lotus and vine leaves. Some of the capitals have tendrils and bunches of grapes combined in interesting variations. Limestone particularly lends itself to deep carving and the resulting contrast of light and shade, which was a stylistic development of Greek art, continued in late antiquity and later in Coptic art. No shafts of the columns were found on site. They were probably taken for re-use in later monuments. It is interesting to learn that the archaeologists excavating this monastery found that the monks themselves had re-used stone from a neighbouring pharaonic burial ground.

The painted niches on the right-hand wall are in an excellent state of preservation. One shows the seated Virgin with the Child on her lap and with Christ painted above them in the dome. The niche in the rear right-hand corner of the chamber shows Mary seated with the child Jesus at her breast. Representation of the suckling of infants has its origin in ancient Egypt: in the Temple of Khonsu, at Karnak, the god Horus is shown at the breast of a goddess, and many scenes on ostraca from Deir el-Medina feature the suckling of infants. Bronze statuettes of the goddess Isis seated with Horus on her lap have also been found in their hundreds throughout Egypt and, indeed, the Hellenistic world.

The sixth century stone pulpit at the centre of the rear wall with a stairway leading up to a cubical, is noteworthy. It resembles the stairs and shrines in the Heb-Sed court of the funerary complex of the pharaoh Zoser, which is situated some five hundred metres away from the monastery on the Sakkara plateau. The proximity of the two structures points to a possible link between their architectural features. However, the pulpit, which has Coptic texts inscribed on the two sides, has a decorative motif in the shape of a shell at the top, which is a Hellenistic symbol.

Chamber G contains miscellaneous stone sculpture that is reminiscent of the Greek-Egyptian heritage. For example, turning to the right there is a small carving of a sphinx between the columns of a Greek temple and, on the right-hand wall, a frieze of the grape harvest. The latter is somewhat crudely executed but reminiscent of scenes of rural activity depicted in the tombs of ancient Egyptian noblemen on the necropolis. It shows, from the left, musicians in the field followed by various stages of collecting and transporting the harvest, ending with a camel (not a donkey as in the ancient tombs — the earliest evidence of camels in Egypt is towards the end of the first century). The persistence of tradition in the early years of Christianity is exemplified in this frieze. It must be remembered that because the people of the Nile valley were largely illiterate, a symbolic scene such as the grape harvest was something they could appreciate because it was an activity that defied political or religious change.

Biblical themes from the Old and New Testament dominate in chamber H. Left of the entrance doorway is a niche showing Abraham and Isaac with the sacrificial lamb, a carving of the enthroned Christ with two angels, and another of three men in a fiery furnace with a fourth man who is probably a saviour. Such themes were common throughout the Roman world but these carvings have a folk simplicity that is typical of Coptic sculpture. All the figures face forwards and have heads that are somewhat large in relation to the bodies. These characteristics are difficult to explain, apart from the obvious inclination of the early Egyptian Christians to move away from the canons and style of Hellenistic art towards a more personal expression of their faith. The objects on the opposite wall are more Coptic in spirit: a relief of the Virgin and Child shows Mary raising an arm from the elbow in a gesture of piety. Another has a central figure that is difficult to identify (it could be Christ), flanked by angels or magi; the feet appear to float above the ground and the figures have halos around their heads.

The reliefs to the rear of this chamber combine the human figure with plant and animal motifs. That is to say, the figures form part of the decorative design, especially friezes of hunters and animals in thickets. Though crude in execution they are, nevertheless, forceful and expressive.

103

On the right-hand wall of chamber I is a large polychrome wall-painting, It shows four figures, representing Adam and Eve in the Garden of Eden, before and after their fall. The two figures to the right show the pair innocent and unashamed. Then, to the left, after having taken of the forbidden fruit, they are covering themselves. The serpent is painted next to Eve and Adam raises his fingers in accusation. This mural comes from the village of Om el-Beregat in the Fayoum and dates to the eleventh century. Also in this chamber are non-figural paintings with decorative geometrical designs in muted colours.

Moving towards the stairway leading upstairs, we come to a large squarish-shaped capital carved in typical Byzantine basketweave, and decorated with the ancient Egyptian lotus and papyrus plants, representing Upper and Lower Egypt, bound together in the symbol of Unity.

Upper floor. Moving clockwise around the first chamber (J) we come to a painted wooden mummy case, which is excellently preserved. It is decorated with a full-length portrait of the deceased who wears a robe to the ankles. Around the head is a floral garland, like the ancient Egyptian "wreath of justification," which became associated with the wreath of thorns by early Christians. Whether the mummy case was from a pagan or Christian burial ground is not clear.

There are several large tapestries in this chamber. They are parts of curtains. One hanging features a dark-skinned, dancing flute player. Beside him is a vertical panel decorated with pairs of warriors and dancing girls and, in the centre, is a rectangle containing three circles, each with a figure of a man on horseback. The other tapestries are woven with dancers, warriors and musical ceremonies. One is a heavy piece, woven of wool and linen, with geometric designs at the edges and peacocks and an animal like a calf at the centre. All the tapestries in this chamber show Hellenistic and Byzantine influence.

Chamber K is devoted totally to fragments of finely woven textiles, which were bands and medallions that decorated clothing in which the deceased was robed before burial. Thanks to the dry climate of Egypt they have been found in large number. Coptic textile makers were extremely versatile and had a wide range of motifs for decoration. They let their creative imagination have full sway and the freshness and vigour of their expression gives the textiles a peculiar and distinctive attraction. The weaving of a sphinx with a human head (right-hand cabinet), is typically Greek-Egyptian. Birds and animals, like lions, hares and dogs, woven into the foliage or surrounded by geometric designs were frequently used. Fish, grapes and peacocks were popular Christian motifs and biblical scenes include a weaving of the Virgin and Child (right-hand cabinet) and a fragment next to it shows three persons with their arms raised in prayer.

The fine silk ecclesiastical robes and stoles in chamber L date to the eighteenth century. The red silk garment is embroidered with silver threads and the twelve disciples are featured with their names written in Arabic. The silk tunic to the left is of exquisite workmanship, and shows Mary, Jesus, the apostles and saints on the front, and Saint George and the dragon on the sleeves. The silk altar-cover to the right, embossed with silver and featuring Saint Damiana at the centre dates to the ninteenth century.

Chamber M contains ivory work and icons. The ivory objects, in cabinets on the right-hand wall, are of two distinct styles: the classical elegance of the Alexandrine style showing a taste for elaborate ornamentation, and rather unrefined ivories that were found in Upper Egypt. The former objects include seals, bracelets and small boxes as well as combs. One of the most noteworthy objects is a comb carved, on the one side, with a scene of the Raising of Lazarus and the Healing of the Blind Man, and on the other side, with two angels holding a garland framing a saint riding a horse. Some of the ivory-work shows festive scenes; in particular, one of the boxes shows well-dressed, elegant ladies in lavish robes. Although Christian principles regarded luxury and a display of vanity as a fault, women of means did not give up their coquetry. A great many exquisite toilet objects have been found among the Coptic antiquities. The panels with Coptic inscriptions should be noted.

They are examples of perfect carving and finish, clearly indicating pride in workmanship. There are also objects that are crude in execution, such as the figurines that may have been made by the monks themselves. They were found in one of the churches of Old Cairo.

The icons in this chamber are mostly of late date, from the seventeenth and eighteenth centuries. They cannot, therefore, be regarded as typically Coptic. Many of them show the saints in stiff postures, bereft of the freshness of early Coptic art and they include scenes of suffering, which is not a local characteristic. An icon with a complex theme that is also un-Egyptian in character is the resurrection of Jesus, who is portrayed as a soldier. Around the empty sepulchre are Roman soldiers, two of them sleeping.

One of the most noteworthy icons depicts Saint Menas on horseback, holding a bridle and spearing a dragon with a spear bearing a cross at the top. This icon, which is on the same side of the chamber as the cabinets containing ivory carvings, is a good example of simple panel painting executed in muted colours. The artist's name and the date of the picture is often inscribed, in Coptic and Arabic, at the bottom of the picture.

The saints most frequently depicted on icons are Saint George, Saint Michael the Archangel, Saint Barbara, Saint Mark the Evangelist, Saint Antony and Saint Paul. To the left of the doorway leading into the next chamber is an icon showing the latter, Saint Antony and Saint Paul, the two great ascetics whose monasteries are near the Red Sea. The direct, front-view faces and large expressive eyes are typical of Coptic art but the execution of the work shows Syrian influence. The daily food of Saint Paul was half a loaf but on the occasion of the visit of Saint Antony, the crow (painted between the two figures) brought a whole loaf of bread.

Several rooms are devoted to a remarkable collection of metal objects of various periods in silver, bronze, copper and iron. They include both religious and secular items. Among the objects of a religious nature are eucharistic vessels and altar furniture, like chalices, spoons and patens, as well as chandeliers, sanctuary lamps and pilgrimage flasks. The secular items include jewelry and a whole range of kitchen utensils, including weights, measures and ladles.

In the first chamber N some elaborately adorned patriarchal staffs dating to the twelfth century are worth noting. Such a staff, which the Copts call 'the staff of authority', is used only for ornamental purposes. The plain silver-headed staff or mace, known as the pastoral staff, is the one carried by the Coptic patriarch and all his bishops on ceremonial occasions.

There is also an excellent collection of crosses. In the middle cabinet on the rear wall is one shaped like the ancient Egyptian *ankh*, and it has a Christian cross in the loop at the top. It is interesting to note that the crucifix is not used on altars of the Coptic Church. A hand-cross, however, is used for ceremonial purposes when the priest blesses the congregation, after which it is always placed flat. Moreover, the fan, or flabellum, which is also displayed here, was used in the earliest church services, although its function is not known with certainty. The elaborate metal book caskets attest to refined production of metalwork in the tenth and eleventh centuries. They were used for protecting the Holy Writ. Later, when copies of the Bible multiplied, it is possible that the delicate, aged originals were sealed in the caskets and regarded as valuable relics.

In the centre of chamber O is a fine statue of a Roman eagle that was found in the fortress of Babylon. This strongest of all birds of prey, reputed for its keen sight and unmatched ability in flight, was adopted by the Roman Empire as a symbol of splendour and grandeur. Moving to the right there are two helmets, one with four gilded crosses. Between them is a decorative candlestick shaped like a dragon. These objects, and the collection of swords and shields in this chamber, recall to mind that despite Egypt's national Coptic movement, the land was, nevertheless, still part of the Byzantine Empire and some of the monastic centres enjoyed gifts from the imperial workshops. The two excellent patriarchal crowns, surmounted by the cross and decorated with semi-precious stones, were gifts from the emperor of Ethiopia to the parent church, the Orthodox Coptic Church.

Entering chamber P and moving to the left, we find huge iron bolts and keys that once belonged to monastery doors, as well as various utilitarian objects made of metal, including musical instruments and bells. On the other side of the room is an interesting collection of surgical instruments, many of them for use in gynaecology and childbirth. They attest to the fact that monastic centres were concerned with the health as well as the spiritual welfare of the neighbouring communities.

Chamber Q has a collection of wall-paintings from churches in Nubia, primarily from Abd el-Nergui and Sebua. The rest are in the old wing. Most of these paintings were brought to Egypt during the salvage operations in Nubia, during the years 1960 to 1971, when the High Dam was being constructed at Aswan. The Nubian wall-paintings can be distinguished from the Coptic in several respects, particularly in the use of muted colours: soft ochres and olive green. Also, the faces tend to be more rounded than the Coptic, and they are painted in flat colour. The eyes are usually much too large for the face, and often have a black line underlining the eye-bag beneath. This is one of the largest collections of early Christian wall-paintings, which is hardly surprising in view of the fact that Christianity in Nubia survived for eight centuries, and that the largest proportion of Nubia's ancient sites were, in fact, Christian.

We are now back in the chamber with the staircase (J), where several show-cases contain manuscripts. Every monastery, indeed it is possible that every church, once had manuscripts. They were written on scrolls of papyrus and sometimes bound into codices, or books. The codex made an appearance in the first century but scrolls existed alongside it for at least two hundred years. In the fourth century the codex took over as the most popular format. Texts on parchment are less common in Egypt due to the availability and durability of papyrus paper. There are also texts on ostraca — pieces of broken pottery — as well as stone, bone, metal and some on wooden tablets. All texts were written with reed pens.

The texts include the biographies and teachings of the early anchorites as well as prayers, sermons, poetry — both religious and profane — magical formulae and popular romances. The bilingual texts are especially noteworthy. One is a tenth century manuscript from the Fayoum, written in both Coptic and Arabic, and vividly adorned in the margins with figures of animals and birds. The manuscripts are bound in embossed leather and adorned with miniature paintings of the saints. One of the cabinets contains magical texts with weird symbols. A large number of these have come to light from several sites, along with amulets and some magicians' hand-books. The intervention of magical powers was sought in a variety of ways among the pre-Christian communities in the Nile valley. These included prayers, curses and even rituals that invoked the help of ancient deities. Egyptian symbols and formulas have been found in all parts of the Mediterranean world and are testimony to the trust placed in magical ritual devised by priests in ancient Egypt who had a great reputation as healers and magicians.

We now descend the stairs, return to the first chamber (A) and enter a porch situated to the right of the entrance doorway. Here there is another collection of funerary stelae that come from various pagan cemeteries throughout Egypt and are believed to date between the second and third centuries. Some of the stelae portray the deceased reclining on a couch holding a drinking vessel, or standing upright in a niche. Often a figure is flanked by the ancient Egyptian gods Horus and Anubis, or by the goddesses Isis and Nephthys. These stelae are historically important because they provide evidence of various styles of Coptic writing, idioms and symbols as well as the names of many towns and villages of Egypt.

Old Wing. This wing contains a large collection of woodwork, panel-paintings and pottery. It was closed during and after the war of 1967 when most of the objects were put in storage, and re-opened in 1983 after complete renovation of the building. The entrance is approached from the garden lying to the left of the new wing. A flight of stairs leads up to the first chamber.

The architectural features of the old wing are worth noting, especially the fine wooden ceilings, arches and tiles that were all collected from old Coptic houses and placed in the structure of the building. The *Mushrebiya* windows are made of finely carved segments made of contrasting woods fixed together without the use of nails or glue, while allowing room between each piece for expansion or contraction of the wood. The building itself and the objects on view are made of a variety of wood. For heavy carpentry the sycamore, acacia, palm and dom trees were used, and for finer work cedar from Lebanon, pine and walnut from Europe and western Asia, and ebony from Africa were popular.

To the left of chamber 1 is the wooden pinewood altar-dome that was brought from the Church of Abu Sarga in Old Cairo. The altar itself is early, dating to the fourth century, but the wooden dome dates to the Fatimid era, the tenth and eleventh centuries. The walls of this chamber, as well as those of the next five chambers, are adorned with framed segments of wall-paintings that were saved from the churches of Nubia, specifically from Abu el- Narki, Abu el-O'da and el-Sebua. As already mentioned, these paintings differ from Coptic wall-paintings, especially in the use of muted colour. There are two *lunettes*, or paintings in half-circles, from Bawit, in chamber 4. It shows three saints with a horseman to the right, honouring them. The figure to the left is believed to be a martyr. There is also a large painting of Jesus, standing and holding the Bible with one hand while making the sign of the benediction with the other.

We now pass into the section of the museum devoted to a rare collection of assorted woodwork dating from the fourth to the end of the seventeenth century. The sanctuary screen from the Church of Saint Barbara in chamber 5 is in sycamore. The panels are carved with biblical scenes including one of Christ and Mary with the apostles and another of Christ and Saint Mark.

Many of the wooden objects are of unknown provenance but probably come from various sites in the Fayoum, Middle and Upper Egypt. Although most of them cannot be dated with certainty they have been grouped according to stylistic sequence. The *first* group of objects, in chamber 6, dates from the fourth to sixth centuries. They are rectangular and square friezes that may have been placed on coffins as decoration as they are not large enough for door-lintels. They are carved with Nilotic vegetation like the lotus and papyrus along with ducks, crocodiles and Hellenistic mythological subjects, like Leda and the swan.

110

Chamber 7 has a cabinet containing wooden panels of the same period but with the human figure combined with the aquatic plants and animals to form the decorative theme. The most interesting object in this chamber is a large panel carving that was found in the Church of Al Moallaka and dates to the fifth century. It shows the triumphal entry of Christ to Jerusalem on Palm Sunday, where He is welcomed by a crowd bearing palm-leaves. The text is in Greek.

The *second* group of objects is in chamber 8. They include wooden panels, which were probably parts of wooden boxes, carved with a wide range of animals and birds — pigeons, peacocks, gazelle and lambs — as well as biblical themes, such as images of the apostles, saints and Jesus Christ. On the right-hand wall is a showcase containing portrait panels from Bawit. They were painted from life and hung on the wall, much as paintings are today. On the death of the individual the naturalistic portrait was removed from the wall, placed over the head of the deceased and bound into the mummy wrappings. Such portraits were either in encaustic, painted with hot wax put on with a scalpel, and a brush used for detail, or in tempera or water-based paint, which was often more simplified in execution. Shops for portraiture were found in the Fayoum and Bawit, and it is possible that they existed elsewhere. General categories of people were painted: old men, old women, young men, young women, and children. This would enable poor people who had lost loved ones to purchase paintings in as near a likeness to the departed as possible. Among the paintings are soldiers with crosses and one has a wreath round his head.

Further along the same wall there is a cabinet featuring a fine toilet box and panels with figures of saints. One carving of Joseph carrying the child Jesus was found in the Monastery of Saint Jeremias at Sakkara. Above the box, a cross is displayed with the crucified Jesus, which is a rare piece, for many reasons. First of all Jesus on the Cross was not a common theme in Egypt. Secondly, Jesus is depicted without a beard, which is rare, and appears only in the early years of Christianity. Finally, the cross is carved with the Horus hawk and the sun disk at the top, and a weeping woman kneeling beneath.

111

In chamber 9, to the left, there are miscellaneous objects including children's toys, seals and wooden combs of different shapes and sizes. The larger combs were used for wool in the manufacture of carpets. The seals were for impressing the sacred bread. There are also tongs, large wooden keys and musical instruments, most of which were found at Sakkara.

The *third* group of objects in the old wing dates to the seventh century and shows increased Byzantine and Persian influence. They include door panels and lintels that feature the Asian elephant and fabulous animals. The objects in chamber 10 are similar but have, in addition, border designs in geometrical patterns. There are also panels of acrobatic and dancing scenes, musical ceremonies with pipers, dancers and musicians as well as hunting scenes, which date to the tenth and eleventh centuries. the *fourth* group has objects which date to the Fatimid period. The doors, lintels and cabinets are in geometric designs of exquisite workmanship. The remarkable taste and skill of Coptic artists was recognised by the Arabs, who recruited the most talented wood-carvers to adorn their mosques. Coptic woodwork differs from Islamic only in the cross as a distinguishing feature. Finally, the *fifth* group of objects date between the thirteenth to seventeenth centuries. The woodwork is totally devoid of iconographic representations. All the designs are geometric and non-figurative.

Chamber 11 contains patriarchal or episcopal chairs of the tenth century and later. The one to the rear has openwork designs and rosettes carved in relief with the cross at the centre. Chamber 12 contains a great door from an unknown monastery. It is probably a sanctuary screen, which had icons at the top. There is also is a small door of very fine workmanship. It was executed by Copts but probably for Muslim patrons, as the cross is disguised by carving it at a slant. Such disguising of motifs can be found in mosques, too, where Coptic labourers split the cross motif down the centre of the vertical arm, so that the half cross on each wall would be discernible only to a Copt. The famous fourth century door of the Church of Saint Barbara can also be seen in this chamber. It was brought to the museum by Simaika to save it from further damage. The bottom part had already been destroyed.

Descending some stairs, we enter chamber 13, which contains pottery that has been divided according to decoration and size, not location. The reason for this is that the study of pottery from the Coptic period is still a relatively unexplored field. Like stone and wood-work, textiles and ivory-work, it is possible to trace some Hellenistic symbols as well as Persian and Egyptian. Wild and domestic animals were painted on some of the jars and the frog, fish and duck are frequent themes, often combined with vines and tendrils. Egypt had an abundance of raw material for pottery manufacture, including alluvial soil, clay and sand, and it is interesting to note that pottery was so abundant and easy to produce that when cereals and honey were sold, the pottery containers were handed over as well. Characteristics of Coptic pottery are the burnished surfaces and variety of shapes. For example, some of the plates are divided into segments for unknown reasons; the ones with circular cavities may be for candles. There are numerous small pots that may have been designed for perfumes and *khol*, black eye decoration. One cabinet has a large number of pilgrim flasks, many of which are decorated with the figure of Saint Menas in relief shown between two kneeling camels. Also on view are the moulds for making the flasks. Some of the flasks have the name of the pilgrim written in either Coptic or Greek. The large, finely decorated pottery placed against the walls were collected from monasteries throughout Egypt where they were used for storage.

The remarkable ceilings in this part of the museum should be noted. They were rescued from abandoned Coptic homes in Old Cairo prior to their demolition and probably date to the early twentieth century. The central dome is painted with a scene of the port of Istanbul where the red slanting roofs of the houses are offset by the ships in port.

Another short flight of stairs leads to chamber 14, which contains numerous pottery fragments with Arabic writing similar to the pottery sherds of Fustat, the first capital before Cairo. The manufacture of pottery during the eleventh to fifteenth centuries is distinguished by the bright, glazed surfaces with a metallic luster. They are ornamented with floral as well as geometric designs and include Christian motifs such as the fish and the cross. The text (either the name of the owner of the workshop or the man who made the vessel) is in Arabic.

Chamber 15 has a small collection of glassware. The glass industry flourished in Alexandria, Wadi Natrun and the Fayoum. Although glass glaze was used in pharaonic times, glass vessels of perfection and beauty only appeared in the Eighteenth Dynasty — perhaps the result of western Asian techniques of glass manufacture. Egyptian glass reached a peak of perfection during the early Christian period, when Alexandria became the centre of the glass industry, and marvellous vases and jars were exported all over the Mediterranean world. The glass was made from quartz mixed with calcium carbonate, to which natron or plant ash was added along with colouring material. The mixture was fused in clay moulds or rolled or flattened into designs that were used for inlay. Sometimes vases, or even tiny figures, were made on a sandy clay core, shaped as desired. There are two such figurines in this small collection: a tiny figure of the Virgin and Child, and a bearded monk.

Gatehouse of the Old Roman fortress. Decending to the lower level of the old wing, we can cross to the gatehouse of the old Roman fortress of Babylon. Excavations and restoration carried out in 1984 revealed that there was once an ancient river harbour about six metres below the present street level. It shows that the course of the river has changed since the foundation of the fortress and now flows some four hundred metres further west. The stairway leads down between the two great Roman towers, above which is the Church of Al Moallaka. The baptistry of the church is constructed above one of the bastions, and its eastern and western extremities rest on the two south-western bastions. Water seepage remains a problem but wooden planks enable one to descend and view the Church of Al Moallaka from below as well as see an ancient wine-press and some remnants of an early church.

The Library in the old wing is still being restored. The director of the museum, Dr. Gawdat Gabra, explained that it will be re-opened before the end of 1986, and that a small gallery for the exhibition of 'new acquisitions' will be opened.

A Centre for Coptic Studies, the first of its kind in the world, will be built on a vacant lot immediately to the north of the new wing. It will have all modern facilities for study and research for the international community of Coptic scholars. Dr. Gabra explained that because the centre will be close to the museum, it will enable specialists in various media to continue to trace stylistic developments of the exhibits whose provinence is unknown. Dr. Gabra explained that the objects may then be rearranged so as to facilitate an understanding of their historical sequence.

(Note: Some of the exhibits are already being moved and may not be in the positions described in this edition.)

Coptic textile, Coptic Museum. Photograph courtesy of Coptic Museum.

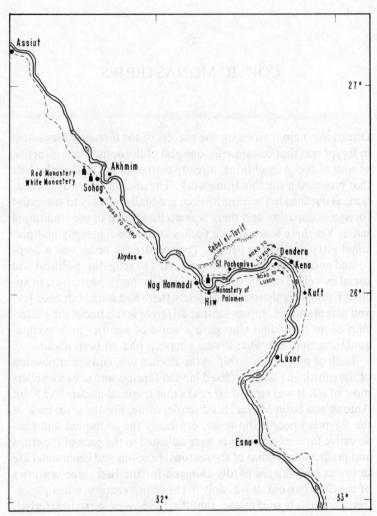

Nag Hammadi and environs

6

COPTIC MONASTERIES

One of the main reasons for the success of the monastic movement in Egypt was that certain religious and philosophical constituents, as well as social conditions, already existed in the land of the Nile that provided a suitable framework. The ancient Egyptian civilisation, as outlined in the introduction, gradually fell prey to successive foreign occupation and there was no leadership in the traditional sense. Yet there was a strong feeling of national identity and personal piety among the people. Their desire for order was a deep-rooted and ancient concept that referred to religious, political and social as well as cosmic order (see *Introduction*). Moreover, in ancient Egypt's highly stratified society there had long been need for, and acceptance of, supervision at different levels under the leadership of an individual who gave a sense of security and spiritual guidance; that was what divine kingship had all been about.

Lack of proper leadership in the Roman era, and the imposition of unrealistic tax laws, affected landed farmers and urban dwellers most of all. It was from their ranks that spiritual leaders like Saint Antony and Saint Makar, his disciple, came. For the great bulk of the Egyptian people, however, especially the soilbound and conservative farmers whose lives were adjusted to the pace of the crops and predictable rhythm of the seasons, religious and ceremonial life in towns and villages hardly changed for the first three centuries of the Christian era. It was only in the fourth century, when paganism was actively suppressed, that their lives were directly affected. The most far-reaching consequence to the official recognition of Christianity as the religion of the Roman empire was the closing of temples. It resulted in a breakdown of religious ritual and the silencing of oracles. Suddenly people had nowhere to turn. It was this vacuum that was filled by the monastic movement.

When Saint Pachom (*chapter two*) decided to unify the wide-spread Christian cenobitic communities and formulate strict rules to govern the daily lives of the monks, he first organised them into a hierarchy. He grouped them by activity, according to their talents, thus providing social stratification and leadership within the monasteries. Leading disciplined lives, the monks brought productivity to the soil, revived crafts and, more importantly, were in communication with non-monastic neighbouring communities. There is abundant evidence in the surviving records of various monasteries, that the monks aided the people economically by providing them with their crop surpluses as well as products from monastic craft industries. Although the monks were looked upon as mortals to whom God had given the power of healing, they nevertheless also supplied medication to those who came for a cure, sought guidance or blessing. The monks even played a role as mediators in popular grievances, whether between members of a single family, or, as was frequent, in disputes over land or water rights between neighbours. In other words, the Pachomian monasteries were not isolated in far-away stretches of the desert but, in many cases, were within easy reach of the valley settlements.

The hard business of survival in desert conditions in Egypt has been somewhat exaggerated; although there is evidence of tens of thousands of ascetics living in the desert, archaeological evidence shows that the caves were often ancient tombs flanking the fertile floodplain, situated near oases in the western desert or located in areas where there were natural springs. Thus, monasteries that were near populated areas provided a restored priesthood which, in a country so much given to religious ritual as Egypt, was extremely important. This is not to say that a monastery was regarded as serving the same function as a temple, but merely that it provided a new focus for worship. Nor did prayers to ancient gods come to an end: "I was the son of a pagan priest," wrote a Copt in the Theban area in the fifth century, "and as a child I watched my father making sacrifice."

Although Pachomian monasticism spread rapidly, large ascetic communities that grew up around spiritual leaders like Saint Antony in the eastern desert and Saint Makar in Wadi Natrun seem, based on architectural and archaeological considerations, not to have followed Pachom's rule but to have continued a semi-cenobitic form of monasticism. The monks only met once a week for mass and a communal meal, followed by a meeting at which work was allocated for the forthcoming week. The rest of the time they could return to their cells or caves to pray or work alone. Saint Pgol, founder of the White Monastery, modified Pachom's rules and introduced a few of his own, such as allowing two monks to share a cell, so that each could report on the pious behaviour of the other.

The Monastery of Saint Jeremias, situated at the edge of the cultivated land at Sakkara, is another notable exception. The site, which was excavated by Dr. P. Grossman of the German Archaeological Institute from 1981 to 1983, covers four acres of land. It may have been the focus of a sprawling community of two thousand monks who lived in surrounding areas. The monastery has a single church that, atypically, has only one apse. Moreover, it is not surrounded by a wall, further supporting the hypothesis that it served a semi-cenobitic community like those of Saint Antony and Saint Makar.

The main areas in Egypt where monasteries are located are: west of the Delta in what was known in early Christian and medieval times as the Desert of Scetis, the Red Sea area in the Gulf of Suez, Middle Egypt and Upper Egypt. Not all of them are inhabited by monks.

THE MONASTERIES OF WADI NATRUN

The famous monasteries of Wadi Natrun lie in a desert depression twenty-five metres below sea level, north-west of the resthouse between Cairo and Alexandria. The name Wadi (valley) Natrun (natron) refers to the vast quantities of sodium obtained from the lake. It was used in ancient times for mummification purposes and in Roman times for glass manufacture.

After the Arab conquest, Wadi Natrun became the official resi-

120

dence of the Coptic patriarch and the number of monasteries grew until there were a reputed one hundred in the area. A great deal of the church literature was translated into the northern Boharic dialect by the monks there and the reputation they thus gained remains to this day.

Wadi Natrun was hardest hit of all the monasteries by the plague in the middle of the fourteenth century and this, combined with frequent bedouin raids, resulted in a sudden decline in the population. The historian al-Makrizi recorded that in the fifteenth century seven monasteries survived in the area. Today there are only four. They can be visited in a single day.

Monastery of Saint Makar (Macarius). Saint Makar, the son of a village priest and disciple of Saint Antony, with whom he lived for many years near the Red Sea, decided to adopt a life of contemplation and prayer around the year 330. The caves in the depression of Wadi Natrun were already inhabited by a large number of ascetics and he, too, lived in a cave. As a result of a divine revelation, however, Makar built a church that became the focus of the community. The Monastery of Saint Makar acquired great distinction in the sixth century when it became the official residence of the Coptic patriarchs. In fact, it takes pride in having supplied no less than thirty patriarchs, more than any other monastery in Egypt.

The churches in the monastery have been destroyed and rebuilt many times in their long history and renovations continue even today. In 1970 the spiritual leader Abuna Matta al-Meskin (Father Matta the Poor One, who revived the anchorite spirit and took to caves in the Wadi el-Rayan in the Fayoum area) settled in Wadi Natrun with a group of hermits. They constructed cells outside the walls of the Monastery of Saint Makar.

The church that bears the name of the patron saint is dedicated to Saint Benjamin and Saint John the Baptist. A second church was built in honour of the forty-nine martyrs who were buried on the site; it contains icons of the three Macarii, Saint Makar, Saint Mark and Saint George, as well as the Holy Virgin. The Church of the Forty-nine Martyrs is used for the liturgy during some Coptic cele-

121

brations, including the feast of the Nativity. This is the occasion when the relics of the three Macarii, and also those of Saint John the Short, are transferred from the Church of Saint Makar to be placed near the choir of the Church of the Forty-Nine Martyrs (chapter two).

The fortress or keep (*kasr* in Arabic) is a three-storied tower. In such towers, which were always constructed near a natural well or spring, the monks could protect themselves when under seige from bedouins. Storage space was usually on the first floor, sleeping accommodation on the second and a chapel, sometimes several, on the third. The keep in the Monastery of Saint Makar is entered by means of a narrow draw-bridge and it has numerous chapels and churches. The one on the first floor, dedicated to the Holy Virgin, has a fine thirteenth century screen. The second floor has chapels dedicated to Saint Michael and to the Saints Antony, Paul and Pachom. On the third floor there is a church dedicated to anchorites, or wanderers, in which nine local hermits are painted on the walls.

Today the monks of the Monastery of Saint Makar collaborate with engineers, agronomists and scientists at Sadat City. They have a modern pump and pump-house as well as tractors. The monastery has thriving agriculture on reclaimed land as well as palm and olive groves. There are about one hundred monks in residence. This is Pachomian monasticism at its finest: pious men with vision and education, combining a life of contemplation and prayer with discipline.

Monastery of the Syrians (Deir el-Suryani). This is one of the leading monasteries of the Wadi Natrun. It was purchased by Syrian merchants at the beginning of the eighth century for the use of Syrian monks. By the eleventh century the monastery could boast of sixty monks. After the plague, which took a terrible toll, the monastery was re-inhabited in the fifteenth century by Syrian and Coptic monks, with the latter element predominent.

The library of the monastery contains over three thousand valuable books and hundreds of manuscripts that are housed in a special building within the complex. Also, a museum contains icons dating to the sixteenth and seventeenth centuries and a twelfth century marble tray from Nubia.

The main church is dedicated to the Holy Virgin and dates to the tenth century. The basin for the foot-washing rite of Maundy Thursday, which is usually located at the entrance of a church, is in the middle of the nave. The sanctuary doors are made of wood and inlaid ivory of particularly fine workmanship. The two central panels of the choir door show Christ and the Virgin. The other panels feature Coptic and Syrian patriarchs as well as Saint Mark the Evangelist and Saint Ignatius, bishop of Antioch. The altar of the church is a slab of black marble that may have been imported by Syrian monks. One of the most important and unusual paintings is in the southern apse. It is a composition of the Annunciation and the Nativity with no separation between the two scenes; the theme of the life of the Virgin, ending with the Assumption, is continued in the other domes.

This church is used during the summer for the celebration of the divine liturgy. During the winter months the monks hold the service in the Church of the Lady Mary, sometimes called the Cave Church, which is one of several lying to the north-east of the monastery.

The Syrian Monastery owns farmland to the north-east and the monks are also active in animal husbandry. Lying between the monastery and the agricultural land is a resthouse where church groups and students are welcome. The monastery is off limits during certain feasts.

Monastery of Saint Bishai. The Monastery of Saint Bishai is joined in a single fortification with the Monastery of the Syrians. Like the latter, it restricts visitors during certain times of the year. The monastery is named after its patron saint who went to Wadi Natrun after a divine revelation and joined the hermit Saint John the Short. The latter had lived alone for many years and suggested that Bishai do

123

likewise, which he did. During the doctrinal disputes between the Melkite and Monophysite monks, both Saint John the Short and Saint Bishai sought refuge with ascetic communities in the area of the Fayoum. In fact, Saint Bishai died in the Fayoum and the monastery in Wadi Natrun that bears his name was only constructed in the seventh century. It contains four churches in addition to the main one built in honour of the patron saint. Saint Bishai's relics were taken there in the ninth century.

Monastery of the Romans (Deir Baramos). This is the most northern of the four monasteries of Wadi Natrun. It is named after Saint Maximum and Saint Domitius, Roman brothers who sought the spiritual guidance of Saint Makar after having served in the Roman army in Syria. The two brothers died a few days apart, and Saint Makar dedicated the cave in which they lived to their memory and built a church near the site. Today the monastery contains five churches: that of the Holy Virgin, that of Saint Theodore, that of Saint George, that of Saint John the Baptist and that of Saint Michael, which is situated on the second floor of the keep. The keep has a drawbridge, secured by what is known as an Egyptian lock: pins that slip into position and which can be lifted by a large wooden key. The refectory, which is not used today, is near the entrance of the main church and contains a refectory table at which the hermits and monks once shared their weekly meal. Leading off the refrectory is the baptistry and a press for making sacramental oil from olives.

The monasteries of Wadi Natrun are large, self-supporting communities that are today enjoying a revival and undergoing expansion. The wells supplying fresh water are as deep as thirty feet. The monks, many of whom are university graduates, are experimenting with agriculture and animal husbandry, introducing new crops and breeds of cattle. They also encourage the development of small craft industries, like weaving and glass manufacturing, which are springing up anew in the area. Over ten thousand people in the town of Wadi Natrun turn to the monks for spiritual guidance.

MONASTERIES OF THE RED SEA

The monasteries of Saint Antony and Saint Paul, in the Gulf of Suez, can be visited in a single day. No permission is required to visit the Saint Antony's monastery and guests are graciously received. If accommodation is required, a letter of introduction from the Coptic patriarchate in Cairo is needed. There is now a new guest wing for visitors, and simple but substantial meals are provided twice a day. In return for this hospitality guests may leave donations in the locked wooden box, and gifts such as tea, sugar, rice or flour are always welcome. Women should wear skirts and preferably a head covering. At the Monastery of Saint Paul accommodation is provided for men only. Women are accommodated at a guest lodge outside the monastery walls. Permission from the patriarchate in Cairo is needed only if more than one night's accommodation is required.

Monastery of Saint Antony. The famous Monastery of Saint Antony lies some 130 kilometres south-east of Cairo, near Zaafarana on the Red Sea coast. It is approached from the desert road that branches off from the Nile valley at el-Wasta, or from the road leading from Suez. It is well supplied with sweet water from three springs and is at present inhabited by about fifty monks.

Saint Antony was born in the village of Koma, near Ehnasia in Middle Egypt towards the middle of the third century and he is said to have died at the age of 105. His parents were fairly well-to-do but as a result of visionary inspiration, he sold his inheritance and gave his money to the poor; he then retreated to the cliffs flanking the Nile valley before eventually settling beneath a range of mountains near the Red Sea known today as the South Kalala (Mount Clysma in Roman times). He became the spiritual leader of a large number of hermits; it was a semi-cenobitic form of monasticism with the monks only meeting once a week for mass and a communal meal, followed by a formal gathering at which work was allocated for the rest of the week. The hermits were otherwise free to return

125

to their cells or caves or to work alone. As Antony's reputation grew, more and more ascetics gravitated towards him and he was obliged to take refuge in a cave 270 metres above the present monastery—680 metres above sea level.

The Monastery of Saint Antony was founded in the fourth century, a few years after the death of the saint, when his followers settled down in the area where their master had lived. It is said that around the year 790 Coptic monks from Wadi Natrun, who had sought refuge at Saint Antony's Monastery during the factional disputes with the Melkites in the fifth century, disguised themselves as Bedouins, entered the monastery and removed the remains of Saint John the Short to take back to Wadi Natrun with them. There were frequent bedouin raids in the eighth and ninth centuries in which the monastery was severely damaged and a great many monks lost their lives. Its history thereafter is uncertain until the twelfth century, when the monastery was rebuilt and adorned with specially commissioned works of art, especially in the Church of Saint Antony. The monastery was again partly destroyed by bedouin tribes in the fifteenth century, when the library was burned, and it was not reoccupied until the end of the sixteenth century after monks from Wadi Natrun had restored the buildings. Most of them date to the seventeenth century and later.

This is one of the most beautiful monasteries in Egypt, largely because of its setting. It is nestled beneath the rugged mountains along the Red Sea coast and is surrounded by high walls of modern construction, over ten metres high in some places. The thickness of the walls provide sentry walks around the top, and there are several watch towers. The guardroom over the gateway has a trap door that was once the only means of access to the monastery; visitors and supplies were hoisted with the aid of a pully. Today the main gate is used.

The oldest part of the monastery is the Church of Saint Antony, which is built over his tomb. The wall-paintings in the narthex and nave are of twelfth or thirteenth century date and include Saint George on horseback and a well-preserved painting of three of the Desert Fathers. Regarded as fine examples of medieval Coptic art, they have recently been restored by the French Institute of Archaeology.

The cave in which Antony took refuge from the thousands of people who came to see him is not visible from the monastery itself. The steep climb is worthwhile as the site commands a magnificent view of the settlement with its fruit trees, palms and vegetable gardens, and the surrounding mountainscape. His cave was situated at the end of a narrow tunnel, approached from a ledge. Below the ledge, a small terrace is said to be the place where he used to sit and weave baskets from palm leaves. He waş kept supplied with provisions by his disciples who came frequently to visit him. The walls of the cave are covered with graffiti, most of which date to medieval times. There are also two panel paintings, one of Christ and one of Saint Antony.

Monastery of Saint Paul. The Monastery of Saint Paul lies about twenty kilometres south of Zaafarana on the Red Sea coast. A signpost marks the road that leads through a twisting and rugged mountainscape towards the secluded haven. Saint Paul was older than Saint Antony who, according to tradition, came to bury him. Unfortunately little was written of Paul in early Coptic sources. He is believed to have retired to the desert at the age of sixteen to escape the persecutions of Decian. The monastery is compact, rectangular in shape and surrounded by high walls. It was founded at the end of the fifth or early sixth century, abandoned in the fifteenth century and only re-colonised in the seventeenth century.

The original entrance through which visitors gained entrance was by means of a pulley, which can still be seen. Today visitors enter a gateway from the south, entering a picturesque village community with fields and domestic animals, mills and a bakery. The monastic buildings are concentrated around the cave where the hermit is believed to have lived in seclusion for eighty years. The Church of Saint Paul was built over this cave where his remains are buried. The wall-paintings are among the earliest in Egypt, believed to date to the fourth century. Inone the Holy Virgin, flanked by angels, holds Jesus and another shows an archangel protecting three youths with his arms. All the figures are frontal and the execution of the work is naive and typically Coptic in spirit. The other three churches in the monastery are dedicated to Saint Mercurius, the Holy Virgin and Saint Michael. The latter is the largest and dates to the seventeenth century.

The water that supplies the monastery comes from "Saint Paul's Spring," which emerges from a crevice in the rock and flows into a cement basin. This, in turn, flows into another basin situated a few metres away. The first is used for drinking and cooking, the second for washing, and a third basin channels the water for irrigating the vegetable gardens, as well as tiny palm groves and an olive plantation.

THE MONASTERIES IN MIDDLE EGYPT

Middle Egypt was once inhabited by thousands of hermits who lived in ancient tombs built in the mountain ranges bordering the floodplain, or founded monasteries within reach of the cultivable land. The most important are the White and Red Monasteries near Sohag, the Monastery of Muharraq in the western desert and the Monastery of Saint Palomen, which is described first because it is situated in an area famous in Coptic history.

Monastery of Palomen (Anba Balamon). This monastery — which is today no more than a group of churches, none of which is ancient — is situated near Hiw, south of Nag Hammadi. It lies within a semi-circle of land about five kilometres in diameter created by the Nile describing a course to the south and then west, before resuming its flow to the north-east. The area is extremely fertile and picturesque, where Christians are numerous to this day.

The monastery can be seen from a distance, its bell-tower with latticed walls rising above the surrounding agricultural land. Within the monastery are three churches, dedicated to Saint Mercurius, Saint Palomen and Saint Damiana. The latter is constructed a metre and a half below the level of the rest of the monastery and is be-

128

lieved to be the most ancient part of the building, but its date is unknown.

Saint Palomen, as already mentioned, was one of the earliest anchorites in Upper Egypt. He was the ascetic who served as a model to Saint Pachom, founder of Pachomian monasticism. The cave of Saint Palomen, whose *mulid* or annual celebration in his honour is still observed, is located in an isolated stretch of desert to the east. This saint was said to have died from excessive fasting and such abstinence may have been one of the reasons why Pachom, when he left the monastery to found one of his own, set down a strict rule to ensure the health as well as the spiritual well-being of his followers.

To the north, beyond the verdure of the valley, rises the Gebel el-Tarif. This range of hills blocks off the horizon from west to east, and it was here that the famous gnostic codices were discovered in 1947. According to one account, a huge boulder had fallen off a slope revealing a jar that was found by peasant farmers. In another account, two brothers chanced upon the jars while they were digging for fertilizer. The codices were believed to have been hidden when the Eastern Roman Church stamped out what they regarded as heretical groups around the year 400. The proximity between two cenobitic communities, one Coptic—distinguished by strict orthodoxy of doctrine—and the other gnostic with their wide range of religious traditions, is interesting; they were undoubtedly aware of one another and, in fact, the Gnostic Literature was translated into Coptic. There may have been strife between the two communities, a suggestion that is supported by a decree issued by Theodore, who succeeded Pachom in 367; he declared that the thirty-ninth letter of Saint Athanasius should be translated into Coptic and read throughout the monasteries of the country. This letter was highly critical of the books written by the Gnostics "to which," he wrote, "they attribute antiquity and give the names of saints."

The White Monastery (near Sohag). This famous monastery was so called because it is built of white limestone. While it once boasted a community of four thousand individuals, today it has no resident

129

monks. The churches, however, are used and several Coptic families live within the enclosure. The monastery was founded in the fourth century by Pgol, a spiritual leader in Middle Egypt who followed Saint Pachom's rules with certain modifications. Each of these modifications was accompanied by an explanatory clause that provided biblical examples for the changes. After the death of Pgol, the monastery was reorganised and enlarged by Saint Shenuda, a religious reformer in Middle Egypt who was extremely strict with the monks. Saint Shenuda was determined to stamp out all forms of pagan worship, especially the worship of relics.

The White Monastery is approached from the Nile valley south of Sohag and, like many monasteries in the Nile valley, it closely resembles an Egyptian temple from a distance, with its sloping walls like an ancient pylon. The Church of Saint Shenuda occupies the largest part of the monastery. It is a fine church with a three-aisled nave and a gallery with freestanding columns, which frame niches that are hollowed out in the semi-circular apses. The main body of the church is decorated with columns surmounted by architraves forming more niches. The deeply cut stonework is characteristic of the fifth century. The church's three vaulted apses are made of fired brick and dedicated to Saint Shenuda, at the centre, with Saint George and the Virgin Mary to each side. The paintings are well-preserved. The one to the south is particularly noteworthy; it shows the Resurrection with the Virgin and angels.

The Red Monastery (also known as Deir el-Bishai). This monastery, which is built of burnt brick, is smaller than the White Monastery and is situated about three kilometres north of it. It was built at the edge of the cultivated land but is today in the midst of the village. Like the White Monastery, it is characterised by great simplicity. It has no resident monks and what were once the narthex and nave of the church are today occupied by several structures of modern date.

The chapel of the Blessed Virgin, in the south-eastern corner, may have been the oldest part of the monastery. But the part of the monastery frequently visited and commented on in medieval times was the Church of Saint Bishai. It is situated at the north-eastern corner and seems to have had many features in common with the church of Saint Shenuda in the White Monastery: the nave and side ailes surmounted by architraves and columns forming niches above, and apses adorned with beautiful wall paintings. The icons on the sanctuary screen are of Saint Shenuda, Saint Bishai and Saint Pgol.

Ruins of the Monastery of Saint Thomas. The ruins of this monastery are situated due west of the town of Sidfa, which is thirty-six kilometres south of Assiut. Although it is fairly remote and difficult of access, it is described here because the whole area around Assiut was once heavily populated with hermitages, and for those of an adventurous spirit who wish to explore the area, with the services of a local guide, such sites as this are recommended.

The ruins of the Monastery of Saint Thomas are located at the mouth of a dried out river bed known as the Wadi Sarga, where a manuscript was discovered describing the community that flourished there in the sixth century. The area was abandoned as a result of frequent raids in the eighth century. It was never re-occupied and, consequently, the wall-paintings were not restored and re-worked as in areas that saw longer occupation. The painting in the dome over the altar features Christ enthroned and also the crowning of the Holy Virgin. This is among the most well-preserved paintings in the early Coptic tradition. There is also a painted panel of Saint Thomas showing the hermit standing and facing forwards with large almond-shaped eyes. His hands clasp beads around his neck, he wears a red tunic and a striped blue and white cloak. This is an icon in the true Coptic tradition.

Deir el-Muharrak. Deir el-Muharrak is the largest and wealthiest monastery in Middle Egypt and is well known for its charitable work among villagers. About ninety monks are in residence, many of them graduates of Cairo and Alexandria Universities.

This is one of the Pachomian monasteries, situated about sixty-five kilometres southwest of Assiut, and is best approached from al-Qusia. Its history is not clear but the monks relate a long-standing tradition that the church of the Blessed Virgin within the monastery was the first church to be built in Egypt and that it was constructed after Saint Mark's arrival in the middle of the first century of the Christian era. Biblical and Coptic traditions are in agreement that the Holy Family left the fertile Nile valley at Qusia (Qusqam of the Bible) and travelled in a south-westerly direction towards Meir and el-Muharrak. There they hid in a cave and Joseph built a small house of bricks and covered it with palm leaves. They lived there for three years, six months and ten days. Biblical historians also agree that it was at el-Muharrak that an angel of the Lord appeared to Joseph in a dream and said, "Arise and take the young child and His Mother, and go into the land of Israel for they are dead which sought the young child's life." (Matt. 2:20).

Deir el-Muharrak has been a place of pilgrimage since early in the Christian era. Medieval and modern historians and travellers alike have been consistent in describing the monastery as a place of healing. During the fast preceding Lent, huge crowds make pilgrimages to the monastery to receive blessing from the monks, to have children baptised or to pray for a cure.

The monastery, which is surrounded by a large, irregularly shaped wall, has two sections, an outer and an inner court. The most ancient part of the monastery lies to the extreme west. This is where the Church of the Blessed Virgin is situated. Its foundations lie more than a metre below the level of the court of the monastery. The altar stone, shaped like an ancient Egyptian stele, bears the date December 11, 747, which is, to the best of our knowledge, a date unconnected with the history of the church. The apse is, according to tradition, built over the original cave where the Holy Family lived.

Above the Church of the Holy Family there was once another church, dedicated to Saint Peter and Saint Paul but only part of the original woodwork remains. It was demolished in the nineteenth century and a new church dedicated to Saint George was built.

The keep is entered by means of a draw-bridge that connects the

132

first floor with a small tower. The church dedicated to Saint Michael, on the second floor of the keep, was built in the sixteenth century. The view from the top of the keep shows a large burial ground extending west of the monastery. An interesting feature is a small extension beyond the wall of the terrace, with a slot in the floor; this served as a toilet in times of attack.

The Monastery of Saint Muharrak has been reconstructed in the modern era. The largest church in the monastery, for example, is the nineteenth century Church of Saint George and the new Church of the Holy Virgin was built in 1964.

THE MONASTERIES SOUTH OF LUXOR

Monastery of the Holy Martyrs (Esna). Esna, the site of the famous ancient Egyptian temple built in Graeco-Roman times, was heavily populated with anchorites and hermitages from the fourth century onwards. This monastery, which is dedicated to 3,600 Egyptian martyrs who refused to offer certificates of sacrifice to the gods in the reign of Decius (249–251), is situated south-west of Esna at the edge of the desert. There are two churches within the enclosure wall. One is a twentieth century construction dedicated to the Holy Virgin, and it is here that permission to visit the other, older church, can be obtained. It was built and dedicated to the martyrs in the year 786 but was reconstructed several times after that date. It contains some fine wall paintings and icons, some in typical Coptic tradition with forward-facing figures and rather primitive execution. Other paintings date to medieval times and were made by pilgrims that came to the area to honour Saint Amon (Amonius), bishop of Esna at the beginning of the fourth century, to whom tradition credits the building of the original monastery.

Monastery of Saint Simeon (Aswan). This monastery is no longer occupied. It lies south-west of the southern tip of Elephantine Island opposite Aswan. It is dedicated to a local saint who lived there in the fifth century. Of its origins we know little. The present construction dates to the seventh century. There is evidence of restoration in the tenth century but the monastery was abandoned in the thirteenth century for unknown reasons. However, lack of water or danger from roving bands of nomads have been suggested as possible causes.

The surrounding wall is over six metres high. The upper part is of sun-dried brick and the lower courses, of hewn stone, are sunk into the rock. At intervals along the wall there are towers. The monastery may originally have been a Roman fortress taken over by the monks and transformed into a monastery.

The cliff face divides the monastery into an upper and a lower level from north to south. The entrance, to the east, leads to the lower level. It has a vaulted central corridor; on the eastern wall is a painting of Christ enthroned with the archangel Michael flanked by six apostles. The small chambers on each side of the corridor contained from six to eight beds for the monks. The upper level, approached by a staircase in the southern angle, is similarly arranged; monks lived in cells opening out on each side of the corridor. At the northern end of the upper level is the main building, which itself is double-storied. The church lies to the southeast between the building itself and the outer wall. The roof was originally a series of domes supported by square pillars. The domed apse at the east has a well-preserved painting of enthroned Christ, His hand raised in benediction. He is flanked by four angels, two of which have wings, long hair and splendid robes. On either side of the recesses are seven seated figures. A cave leading off the northwest corner of the chapel is believed to have been the dwelling place of the patron saint. It has painted walls and a decorated ceiling.

The northern wall of the upper level of the monastery is built over the enclosure wall, with windows looking over the steep cliff. Below the main building are some rock-hewn cells and a rock-chapel painted with saints.

THE SHRINE OF ST. MENAS

The fabled city of Saint Menas is situated in Maryut (Mareotis) which lies in the desert south-west of Alexandria and north-west of Wadi Natrun. The shrine of the saint was one of the great centres of pilgrimage during the fifth to seventh centuries. It was famous as a place of healing and thousands of people travelled there from all over the Christian world, taking home with them sacred water in tiny pottery ampulla in the shape of a flat, two-handled jug.

The city of Saint Menas was described by an Arab geographer, el-Bekri, in the eleventh century, and also by numerous medieval historians and pilgrims. They wrote of superb buildings decorated with statues and mosaics, situated in a fertile region that had vineyards. Numerous modern scholars went in search of the site, but despite clues provided in medieval writings, all trace of the "city" was lost. It was thought to be a legendary place until 1905 when it was discovered by German archeologist Kaufmann. At first it was not clear that the ruined site was, in fact, the city of Menas. Discovery of the tomb of the saint dispelled all doubt. Thirty marble stairs led down to a crypt and the tomb of Saint Menas lay some ten metres under the high altar of the ruins of the original church. In the tomb was an icon of the saint exactly as el-Bekri had described it: a Roman officer standing between two kneeling camels. The excavators also found a potter's workshop where souvenir objects including jugs, lamps and flasks, had been fired 1,500 years earlier for sale to pilgrims.

Saint Menas is said to have suffered martyrdom in 296 when the soles of his feet were torn off, his eyes were gouged and his tongue dragged out by the roots in the reign of Maximianus. Despite these terrible mutilations, Menas was yet able to stand up and address spectators. Finally, the emperor himself slew him and set his body adrift on the Mediterranean in an iron coffin. It was said to have been cast ashore and loaded onto a camel by some passing Bedouins. They proceeded with it into the desert but when the camel reached a certain place in the desert, it refused to move further. It

135

was there that the coffin with the body of Saint Menas was buried.

The basilica constructed over the burial place of the saint has been attributed to the emperor Arcadius (395–408). The builders, patronised as they were by the Eastern Roman Empire spared nothing in its construction. Subsequent emperors erected a second building and a great cathedral was built over the crypt.

After the Arab conquest and the Byzantine withdrawal from Egypt, the shrine of Saint Menas was in the hands of the Greek Orthodox Church. During subsequent disputes between the Greek Orthodox and the Coptic Orthodox Churches on the question of jurisdiction, the site was pillaged and the stone, including valuable marble, taken for re-use elsewhere. In the eighth century the government decreed that the shrine belonged to the Copts. Unfortunately frequent bedouin raids resulted in further desecration of the site.

The Coptic community of Egypt is anxious to resurrect the ancient glory of the city. The saint holds a special place in their hearts. Certainly many of the miracles that Saint Menas was said to have performed — thirteen in number — closely resemble the ancient Egyptian myth of Osiris. Saint Menas was said to have restored to life a man who had been cut to pieces by desert tribes, and also to have joined the parts of the body of an unfortunate man who had been chewed by a crocodile. The joining together of the parts of a dismembered body is, of course, reminiscent of the myth of Osiris, who had been cut into pieces by his jealous brother Set. And the body of Osiris, too, had been sealed in a coffin and cast on water.

Although oral traditions may undergo such drastic change with the passage of time that their origins are lost, and although many myths and legends are almost unrecognisable in their altered context, they yet survive. A highly religious society does not suddenly change. In the words of Peter Brown in his *The Making of Late Antiquity*, we are dealing with a very old world in which "changes did not come as disturbing visitations from outside; they happened all the more forcibly for having been pieced together from ancient and familiar materials." This was doubtless the reason for the rapid spread of Christianity in Egypt, the success of the monastic movement, and the widespread reverence for the Holy Family.

FOR FURTHER READING

Abbott, N. *The Monasteries of the Fayoum*. University of Chicago, Chicago, 1937.

Badawy, Alexander. *Coptic Art and Archaeology*. Cambridge, Mass., 1978.

_____. *History of Eastern Christianity*. Rev.ed. 1980.

Butler, Alfred J. *The Ancient Coptic Churches of Egypt*. 2 vols. Clarendon Press, Oxford, 1884. New ed. 1970

Brown, Peter. *The Making of Late Antiquity*. Harvard University Press, Cambridge, Mass. and London, England, 1978.

_____. *The Cult of the Saints, Its Rise and Function in Latin Christianity*. University of Chicago Press, 1981.

Brooklyn Institute of Arts and Science Museum. *Late Egyptian and Coptic Art*. Brooklyn, New York, rep. 1974.

Dodds, E.R. *Pagan and Christian in an Age of Anxiety*. W.W. Norton & Co., New York, London, 1970.

Evelyn-White, Hugh G. *The History of the Monasteries of the Wadi Natrun*. The Metropolitan Museum of Art, Egyptian Expedition. Cambridge University Press, 1933.

Gerspach, M. *Coptic Textile Designs*. Dover Pub. Inc., New York, 1975.

Hanna, Shenouda. *The Coptic Church, Symbolism and Iconography*. C. Tsoumas, Cairo, 1962.

Hardy, Edward R. *Christian Egypt*. Oxford University Press, Oxford, 1952.

Jonas, Hans. *The Gnostic Religion: The Message of the Alien God and the Beginnings of Christianity*. Beacon Press, Boston, 1958. 2d. ed. 1963.

Lane, Edward W. *The Manners and Customs of the Modern Egyptians*. London: East-West Publications, 1978.

Leeder, S.H. *Modern Sons of Pharaohs, A Study of the Manners and Customs of the Copts of Egypt*. Hodder & Stoughton, London, 1918.

Meinardus, Otto. *Monks and Monasteries of the Eastern Desert*. The American University in Cairo Press, 1961.

137

_____. *Christian Egypt, Ancient and Modern*. 2d ed. The American University in Cairo Press, 1977.

_____. *Christian Egypt Faith and Life*. French Institute of Oriental Archaeology, Cairo, 1970.

Montet, P. *L'Egypte et la Bible*. Neuchatel, 1959.

Oesterley, W.O.E. *The Wisdom of Egypt and the Old Testament*. London, 1927.

Peet, T.E. *Egypt and the Old Testament*. Liverpool, London, 1922.

Robinson, James M. Introduction in *The Nag Hammadi Library in English*. E.J. Brill, Leiden, 1977. Evanston, New York and Harper & Row, San Francisco, 1977.

Robinson, James M. *The Coptic Gnostic Library: with English Translation, Introduction and Notes*. E.J. Brill, Leiden, 1975ff.

Sugden, E.H. *Israel's Debt to Egypt*, London, 1928.

Watkin, Edward. *A Lonely Minority. The Modern Story of Egypt's Copts*. Wm. Morrow & Co., New York, 1963.

Worrell, Wm.H. *A Short Account of the Copts*. University of Michigan Press, Ann Arbor, 1945.

INDEX

139

See also Coptic Church
Arians: and theological disputes, 42, 44; status in Roman Empire, 46. See also Constantius
Arius, 42, 43, 44
Armenia, 43
Arsinoë, 47-48
Art: Alexandrine, 71, 75, 96, 105; Byzantine, 70, 73, 75, 78; Greek inspired, 68, 69, 70, 76, 96, 102, 104, 105, 113; Persian-inspired, 112, 113; of Rome, 70, 71, 78, 94, 103; Syrian, 69, 70, 75, 78, 79, 106
—objects from: Antioch, 70; Asia, 110; Bawit, 71, 73, 77, 101, 110, 111; Church of al-Moallaka, 85, 111; Church of Saint Barbara, 110, 112; Church of Saint Sergius, 85, 110; Constantinople, 70, 71, 78, 96; Monastery of Saint Jeremais, 77, 101, 111; Nubia, 108, 110; Old Cairo, 79, 106, 113; Upper Egypt, 71-72, 105, 110
—of: Saint Antony, 106, 127; Saint Makar, 121; Saint Mark, 106, 110, 121, 123; Saint Menas, 71, 106, 113; Saint Paul, 86, 106. See also Coptic (script); Coptic Museum; Cross; Fayoum; Saint George; Holy Virgin; Jesus
Ashmounein, 62
Asia: and Council of Nicea, 43; and glass manufacture, 114; mercenary troops from, 19; monastic movement in, 50; and Romans, 27; and saints, 62, 86; Serapis cult in, 20; and trade with Egypt, 19. See also Nicomedia
Assiut, 54, 62, 131
Assyria, 16-17, 43
Aswan (Syene), 27: and Elephantine Island, 22-23, 134; High Dam at, 108; and Monastery of Saint Simeon, 77, 133-134; Roman garrisons at, 27
Aten (hymn to), 41
Athanasius, Saint, 44-45, 46, 50;

at Council of Nicea, 43-44; and Ethiopian church, 50; thirty-ninth letter of, 129; and Nicene creed, 43-44, 49, 51; and Saint Antony, 45, 46, 48
Augustus, 27
Aurora, 29
Ayyubid Dynasty, 51

Babylon. See Old Cairo
Babylon (of the Euphrates), 81
Bacchus (god), 68
Bacchus (martyr), 87
Bagawat (Kharga Oasis), 48, 49, 77
Baghdady, 79
Bahnasa: bishop of, 48; and Holy Family, 61, 62; New Testament writings from, 33; and Oxyrhynchus, 61
al-Bahnasa (oases): shrine at, 62
Bahr Youssef, 61
Bahriyah Oasis, 62
Bakhum, Anba. See Pachom, Saint
al-Bakir, Mohammed, 61
Balamon, Anba. See Palomen, Saint
Barbara, Saint, 92, 106
Basil, Saint, 50
Bawit: art objects from, 71, 73, 74, 77, 101, 110, 111; portraiture shops in, 106
Bedouin(s): and Coptic monks, 126; raids of, 75, 121, 122, 126, 131, 134; and Saint Menas, 135, 136
el-Bekri, 135
Ben Ezra, Abraham, 93
Benedict, Saint, 50
Beni Mazar, 61
Beni Suef, 64, 96
Benjamin, Saint, 121
Bible: copies of, 107, on Holy Family in Egypt, 62; Latin translation of, 50; in painting, 110; and Qusqam, 64, 132. See also Scriptures
Bilbais, 61
Bishai, Saint, 123-24, 131
Black Sea, 43

141

142

culture, 19, 20-22, 102; scholars, 18; under Romans in Egypt, 27, 28, 45. *See also* Ptolemies

Greek (script): in Coptic art, 68, 69, 110, 113; in Coptic hymns, 55; in Coptic manuscripts, 76; and Coptic script, 22; under Diocletian, 38; in ecclesiastical literature, 20; literature translated into, 21, 23; spoken by Egyptian Jews, 22

Grossman, Peter, 101-2, 120

Hades, 21
Hadrian, 28
Hamanout, Saint Takla, 77, 86
Hanging Church. *See* Church of al-Moallaka
Hathor, 28, 47, 55, 63, 74
Hebrew, 23
Heb-Sed court, 102
Hecateaus (of Miletus), 18
Heliopolis, 61
Hermopolis, 19, 62
Hera, 20
Hermes, 21
Hermes Trismegistus. *See* Thoth
Hermetica. *See Corpus Hermeticum*
Heracleopolis Magna, 43
Hercules, 68
Herod, 27
Herodotus, 18, 25
Hierakleopolis. *See* Ehnasia
High Dam (Aswan), 108
High Priest of Alexandria and all Egypt (Old Kingdom), 29, 70
Hikaptah. See Memphis
Historia Lausica, 48
Hiw, 128
Holy Family: Egyptians' reverence of, 59, 136; and Flight to Egypt, 59, 61-62, 87, 91, 132; icon of, 91. *See also* Jesus; Joseph; Holy Virgin
Holy Ghost, 69. *See also* Trinity
Holy Virgin: appearances of, in Old Cairo,

58; Annunciation of, 78, 123; Assumption of, 58; 123; chapels dedicated to, 122, 130; depicted in churches and monasteries, 55, 60, 86, 87, 91, 92, 121, 123, 127-28, 130, 131; in Coptic art, 74, 76, 77, 101, 102, 103, 110, 114; and Flight into Egypt, 59, 60, 61, 62, 132; similarity to Isis, 60. *See also* Church of the Holy Virgin; Church of the Lady Mary; Church of the Lady Palm; Holy Family

Holy Week, 57
Honorius, 46
Horus, 21, 30: in art, 69, 96, 102, 109, 111; New Year festival of, 63

Ignatius, Saint, 123
Incarnation (New Testament), 42
India, 26
Insinger Papyrus, 33-35
Instruction Literature, 22, 33-35, 72
Ireland, 50
Isaac (Old Testament), 103
Ishnin al-Nasarah, 48
Isis: in art, 96, 102, 109; influence on Coptic Christianity, 29; cult of, in Graeco-Roman world, 30; and Demeter, 21; festival of, in Rome, 30; similarity to Holy Virgin, 60; in Osiris myth, 29-30; temple of, at Philae, 22, 29, 30
Islam, 51, 57, 75. *See also* Koran; Mohammed; Muslim(s)
Israel, 62, 132
Istanbul, 113

Jerome, Saint, 41, 47, 48, 50
Jerusalem, 22-23, 43, 93, 111
Jesus (Christ): and Arabic script, 61; Ascension of, 58; depicted beardless, 111; birthplace of, 70; depicted in churches and monasteries, 60, 86, 87, 91, 92, 110, 123, 127-28, 130, 131, 134;

144

145

Maryut, 135

Maspero, Gaston, 74

Masr el Qadima. See Old Cairo

Mataria, 61

Matta al-Meskin, Abuna, 121

Maundy Thursday, 84, 123

Maximian, 87

Maximianus, 39, 71, 135

Maximum, Saint, 124

Medinet Habu, 47, 73, 74

Meir, 62, 132

Melkites: influence on Coptic art, 70; and Copts, 75, 126; Egypt's political opposition to, 49; and Monophysites, 49-50, 124; and patriarchs, 50, 51; and Saint Catherine's Monastery, 78

Memnon, 29

Memphis: Arab-Egyptian discussions in, 51; Assyrian invasion of, 16; as capital of ancient Egypt, ix; cults in, 20; under Ptolemies, 21, 24; and Saint Sophia, 38

Menas, Saint, 135-36

Mercurius, Saint, 94

Metternich stelae, 69

Michael (archangel), 69, 86, 106, 134

Michael, Saint, 56, 106, 122

Middle Egypt: carvings from, 96; cities in, 19, 96, 125; Copts in, 54; hermits in, 39, 128; Holy Family in, 59, 61; monasteries in, 48, 74, 96, 120, 128, 131; New Testament writings from, 33; pilgrimage in, 60; and saints, 125, 130

Miletus, 18

Mohammed (Prophet), 59

Monastery of Saint Antony, 125-27

Monastery of Saint Apollo, 74, 77

Monastery of Saint Bishai, 123-24

Monastery of Saint Jeremias, 74, 120

Monastery of Saint Makar (Macarius), 54, 63, 77, 121-22. *See also* Makar, Saint

Monastery of Saint Muharrak. *See* Deir el-Muharrak

Monastery of Saint Palomen, 128-29

Monastery of Saint Paul, 125, 127-28

Monastery of the Romans, 124

Monastery of Saint Simeon, 77, 133-34

Monastery of the Syrians, 71, 75, 122-23

Monastery of Saint Thomas, 131

Monophysites, 42, 45, 46, 49-50, 75

Moses (Old Testament), 23, 59, 93

Mosque of Amr, 94

Mubarak, Hosni, 54

al-Muharrak. *See* Deir el-Muharrak

Munster University, xi

Museum(s): British, 71; Brooklyn, xi; Cairo, 95; Graeco-Roman (Alexandria), 95; Islamic (Cairo), 95; of Pharaonic Antiquities (Boulac), 74; Ravenna, 71. *See* Coptic Museum

Museum, the (Alexandria), 21, 27

Mushrebiya, 109

Muslim(s), 55, 58-59, 61, 71, 112. *See also* Islam; Mohammed; Ramadan

Mut, 20

Myriam. *See* Holy Virgin

Nag Hammadi, 39, 40, 128; library of, 35-36, 64

Nagada, 54

el-Nassikh, John, 79

Nativity, 77, 78, 122, 123

Naucratis, 19

Nebuchadnezzar, 23

Negative Confession, 63-64

Nepthys, 30, 96, 109

Nero, 28, 33

New Rome. *See* Constantinople

New Testament: translated into Coptic, 47; themes from, in Coptic Museum, 103; Raising of Lazarus, 105; in Nag Hammadi library, 36; writings of, in Bahnasa, 33

Nicene creed: Christians' adherence to, 44; and Copts, 50, 51; and Council of Nicea, 46-47; doctrine of, 52; and Monophysites, 49

146